BEING A
SINGER

BEING A SINGER

The ART, CRAFT, and SCIENCE

LINDA BALLIRO

Foreword by JACK CANFIELD

CHICAGO
REVIEW
PRESS

An A Cappella Book

Access recordings at **www.lindaballiro.com**

Published by Chicago Review Press Incorporated
814 North Franklin Street
Chicago, Illinois 60610
ISBN 978-1-64160-204-4

Library of Congress Cataloging-in-Publication Data
Names: Balliro, Linda, 1962- author.
Title: Being a singer : the art, craft, and science / Linda Balliro ;
   foreword by Jack Canfield.
Description: Chicago, Illinois : Chicago Review Press, [2019] | Includes
   bibliographical references and index.
Identifiers: LCCN 2019014853 (print) | LCCN 2019015454 (ebook) | ISBN
   9781641602051 (adobe pdf) | ISBN 9781641602075 (epub) | ISBN 9781641602068
   (kindle) | ISBN 9781641602044 (trade paper)
Subjects: LCSH: Singing—Instruction and study.
Classification: LCC MT820 (ebook) | LCC MT820 .B18 2019 (print) | DDC
   783/.043—dc23
LC record available at https://lccn.loc.gov/2019014853

Cover design: Preston Pisellini
Interior design: Jonathan Hahn

Printed in the United States of America
5 4 3 2 1

In memory of Dr. James Martin Balliro, MD,
who taught me to play chess and pay attention to details.

CONTENTS

FOREWORD

There are two things that will make you wise: the books you read and the people you meet. *Being A Singer: The Art, Craft, and Science* is one of those books. It's more than voice training—it will empower you to reach your highest vision of being a singer.

I know a little about this because I've been teaching and training people for decades to develop concrete visions of their dreams *and* learn the tools they need to achieve them. *Being A Singer: The Art, Craft, and Science* holds the same strategy I use to teach people to find their soul's purpose: use your mind, learn the tools, and take action.

I began writing the first *Chicken Soup for the Soul* book because I wanted to be a teacher with a capital *T* for the whole planet. I remember writing from 10:00 PM to 1:00 AM every night for a year to finish that book, then brainstorming the title for weeks, then pitching the book all over Manhattan in a wild three-day pitch marathon; 144 publishers rejected the book. So, when I met Linda Balliro, associate professor of voice at Berklee College of Music, and heard about *Being A Singer: The Art, Craft, and Science*, I understood the challenges she faced writing and getting her first book published.

I also understood that reading this book can *change* your life. Similar to the way that *Chicken Soup for the Soul* provided my readers with inspiration and tools to find their purpose and transform their lives, this book provides you with legendary vocal training, knowledge, and inspiration so you can find your voice and achieve the transformations you need for your life and work. You'll be inspired, informed, and pushed out of your comfort zone with an experienced teacher supporting and guiding you every step of the way.

Another reason I am excited about and feel close to this book has to do with my youngest son. From the moment my children were born, I've been dedicated to supporting them in pursuing and fulfilling their souls' purpose, which includes doing anything I can to get them the training and the tools they need. All three of my sons have pursued careers in music, and that's why my youngest son, Christopher, is currently a voice student at the Berklee College of Music. The teachers at Berklee are the best in the world.

As I tell all my children and students, you were born with the talent and the power to achieve greatness and create anything and everything you want in life, but you have to take the right actions to make it happen. This book will help you do that.

Enjoy the journey.

—JACK CANFIELD

Cocreator of the Chicken Soup for the Soul series
Coauthor of *The Success Principles: How to Get from Where You Are to Where You Want to Be*

INTRODUCTION

It's pretty tough to learn to sing from a book. Many singers who've tried have come to me for voice training. Although some of the self-study materials they used included good training materials, they were all confused about how to use their voices. They sang with tension, reached for high notes, had tuning problems, were unable to control dynamics, and couldn't communicate the message of the music.

Before writing this book, I saw a video review on Amazon made by a young singer who had purchased a singing book. The book showed exercises and a "method" for singing. He had recorded himself singing when he received the book, and then again after practicing the exercises for three months. In the first video, he has a typical beginner's voice: soft, not much range, a little wobbly on pitch, but basically a pleasant sound with a nice sense of the words and an authentic presence. In the second video, after three months of practicing on his own using the exercises in the book, his sound was forced and dull with no resonance, his swallowing muscles were bulging from his neck, his face reddened, and he looked totally stressed out. His pitch inconsistencies hadn't improved; they had gotten worse. He'd lost his pleasant sound and authentic connection to the lyrics. Instead of improving his understanding and skills, he'd developed motor skills and perceptions that would take a long time to rehabilitate. And because of muscle tension, he'd lost his own voice—the qualities that gave his voice identity. He wasn't aware of what had happened to his voice. Sadly, he thought he had improved because the sound seemed louder. I worried about this poor singer for days.

I won't let this happen to you, just like I won't let it happen to any of the singers I work with in person. I made that commitment when I began teaching, and I made it again when I set out to write this book.

The book you're holding in your hands is built on the voice training approach of Seth Riggs and my own experience applying his training approach with thousands of singers, including nationally touring professionals, students, preteens, and recreational singers of all ages. Riggs developed his approach from his studies with master teachers who were descendants of the finest teachers of the fifteenth through nineteenth centuries, and by training many of the great singers of the twentieth century in contemporary music, opera, and musical theater.[1]

I began studying with Seth after years of performing classical music in Central Europe. Twenty years earlier, I had graduated from New England Conservatory in Boston, sold everything I owned, and moved to Europe. I planned to study in Europe for a year and then return to the United States for graduate study, but I got addicted to pounding the pavement, developing my craft, and the European café lifestyle, so I stayed for thirteen years. After years of singing Mozart and Schubert, with many American art song recital tours in between, I still felt like I was missing something. Auditioning was difficult because I felt like some days my voice sounded great and everything was easy, and some days

it wasn't! Nevertheless, I was performing and auditioning while I continued searching for a teacher or coach who could help me solve the puzzle. That's when I met Seth Riggs. After graduating from a prestigious conservatory and years on the road singing the music of Mozart and Schubert, I found myself putting together the pieces of the puzzle with Michael Jackson's voice teacher! It didn't make any sense!

But I soon realized that Seth Riggs's training of hundreds of celebrities is only the headline. The in-depth story is the *approach* that allowed him to build the voices of celebrities, industry professionals, and everyday singers and teachers. Under the tutelage of Seth Riggs and his protégés it became apparent that training the coordination of vocal registers, areas of the voice that have similar acoustic and mechanical properties, is a robust key to unlocking the power, flexibility, and expression of the voice. No matter what style of music you sing—no matter what kind of voice you have—when you've mastered the craft of moving from low to high in your voice, without "reaching" for notes or blowing air to hide problem zones, you have unlimited choices. And I was also pleased to have found a master teacher who also loved the songs of Roger Quilter—we had a great time singing them together!

Consider my education and background as a unique lens converging a spotlight on this legendary training. I grew up listening to my parents' recordings of the

Rat Pack (Dean Martin, Sammy Davis Jr., Frank Sinatra) and the great popular singers of the movie musical genre like Judy Garland and Barbra Streisand. After teaching myself to read music on the piano, I studied classical piano for ten years and then began studying with a jazz piano teacher. (He wouldn't let me touch the keys until I had studied theory for two months!) I sang in school shows, performing solo from the age of eight, then performing musical theater throughout high school. There were also dance lessons at the Boston Ballet School for children, modern dance in college, and intensive acting training at prestigious theaters in Boston. Between the ages of nine and eleven, I toured local churches with a guitarist singing Christian folk music for ceremonies and masses, getting my first "paychecks."

Then, after years of studying and performing classical music, and years studying the pedagogy of contemporary singing with Seth Riggs and a few of his best protégés, I became an associate professor at Berklee College of Music. Berklee stands as the perfect "voice teacher's laboratory" where a voice teacher must synthesize theory with high-pressure demands from *daily* performing, rehearsals, recordings, and auditions to quickly and effectively solve vocal challenges. My teaching skills have been seasoned by training these young voices who are under intense pressure. At the same time, I've been training private students from all genres, includ-

ing experienced opera singers, nationally touring contemporary artists, extraordinary kids and teens, and recreational singers. This work allows me to keep my finger on the pulse of the "real world" of singing, auditioning, and performing.

In the following pages, you'll find vocal training that reaches across the ages and has endured decades, and even centuries, of cultural shifts and musical evolution. Elucidated by current research in vocal science, acoustics, and cognition, along with stories and interviews from industry pros, and exercises to chart your experiences, you won't get "stuck" or lost in the ether of mysterious jargon. The work you do with this material will propel you forward to a new level of awareness and mastery.

This book was written in response to the unprecedented degree of pressure on singers today. We're in the midst of a "perfect storm" that's creating an urgent need for tools that solve today's challenges without diluting proven approaches of the past. Colleges, universities, and conservatories are training singers by the thousands, television reality shows like *The Voice* and *American Idol* have record-breaking TV ratings all over the world, expensive opera and Broadway musicals play to sold-out audiences, the Metropolitan Opera broadcasts live in movie theaters, and we have an endless stream of online music. Singing has become omnipresent in our lives. You have more opportunities to sing and be heard than ever before. At the same time, the fields of vocal science and neuroscience have stepped into their "golden age"—new and deeper understandings of how the voice, mind, and body function emerge every day. There's an extraordinary amount of information available to everyone online, in books, in every vocal studio on every street corner.

Despite this unparalleled accessibility, many singers are confused and frustrated. *Quantity* of information doesn't provide solutions—it creates confusion. At the same time, our twenty-first-century, high-tech, fast-paced culture demands that singers evoke more and more powerful emotional responses based primarily on volume and stage spectacle, creating a heavy burden on singers' bodies, minds, and voices. Singers must be able to easily sing many styles, perform in cavernous venues, compete with technology, and manage fast-paced tours with demanding travel schedules. In recording studios, a producer focuses on the sound and feel of the music, but not the singer's voice and body, so when a singer gets hoarse halfway through the recording session, then that's the producer's final take because the singer's exhaustion creates a "vibe." More than any other time in history, singers must develop reliable, consistent, flexible, and powerful voices, regardless of genre or style. No matter how much talent you have, without training your ability to move easily from low to high and back again, without crafting *how* you use your voice,

mind, and body, you may collapse under the weight of these demands. The need for training has never been more urgent than it is today.

If you want to survive and thrive as a singer, you need powerful tools. You already have the most powerful; just like Dorothy in *The Wizard of Oz*, you have your own experience and intuition to show you the way. You can develop both of them right here and now by becoming brutally honest with yourself. Take this chance to examine your singing and step outside your comfort zone. Use the tools, strategies, and insights in this book to develop the voice you want. What aspects of your singing do you want to change? What discomfort, pain, or hoarseness are you tolerating? Are your instincts being nurtured, or are they shut down by the people and information around you? What tools do you have? Which great singers are you listening to? More than anything else, *your own experience while singing* informs your voice, mind, and body. Ultimately, this is what leads you to free and expressive singing.

I know that singing is an integral part of your identity. When you're struggling with it, that struggle can affect every aspect of your life and work. As a teacher, I've seen singers in a lot of distress when they're not happy with their singing—afraid, embarrassed, and frustrated, they start believing they don't have what it takes to be a singer, thinking that no one else has these problems, worried they don't sound "beautiful," or feeling that they can't express what they want to say. I'm grateful that I've been able to train thousands of people to sing easily throughout their range and develop the power, flexibility, and expressiveness they need. And now I'm committed to helping you too.

Maybe you've just begun singing and you need a road map. Or maybe you're already singing in summer programs, gigs, concert performances, tours, or studio recordings, but you feel like you're missing something. Maybe you're lacking confidence, frustrated, or just wondering if you can do more. If your voice is sometimes hoarse, inconsistent, or unreliable, if you're unable to use dynamics throughout your range, if high notes require too much effort, then you know there's more you can achieve.

I know you've chosen this book because you're ready to face your challenges and develop the voice you deserve. I want you to know you won't be doing it alone.

You can start right now by defining and trusting your own experience. Your memories of how singing *feels* and your intuition must stay with you throughout your training, not your fears or belief systems. Believe in your own experience and proceed with courage. You have the wisdom of the ages in this book, and in your own voice, mind, and body.

BEING A SINGER

PART I

How Your Singing Functions

MOBILIZE YOUR VOICE, MIND, AND BODY

He told me I had a diamond in my throat, but that
it needed polishing to remove the carbon it still bore.

—Birgit Nilsson, *My Memoirs in Pictures*[1]

When I entered New England Conservatory of Music as an undergraduate student, I had already been singing in schools and churches for years. I began doing church "gigs" for special events at eight years old and toured my local area for a few years. Then I went on to various shows, concerts, and events throughout my teens. But I felt like something was missing. I had a voice, but I sensed that great singers were doing a few things I couldn't do. I thought I would study at the conservatory, learn everything I needed, and then live happily ever after. As it turned out, it was a bit more complicated than that, but my education, training, performing, and teaching have been a great adventure. Each experience opens new doors that I didn't even know existed, and there isn't an end in sight.

While I was a student, I read many singer biographies because I wanted to know behind-the-scenes details. How did great singers learn? Where did they study?

3

Did they face any challenges? When I read *My Memoirs in Pictures*, the quote above inspired me to forge ahead, but I didn't really understand how much of an impact the idea had on me until I started writing this book.

Birgit Nilsson (1918–2005) was a highly acclaimed international opera singer. She had a tremendous career singing dramatic roles in Wagner, Puccini, and Verdi operas because her voice was a powerful force, with ringing high notes and an intuitive sense of drama. She sang an impressive "debut" concert in Stockholm when she was very young, but after the concert Isaac Grünewald, one of Sweden's most famous painters, said her voice needed "polishing." What? Such an impressive talent and gifted voice with a sensibility for music! Couldn't she just study music, get some experience, and become a star?

Not exactly. Like so many stars and celebrities, she appeared to have a meteoric rise to success. In reality, she struggled with her training for several years, was frustrated with her studies, and juggled money to pay for her lessons. Sound familiar? Despite it all, she was determined to develop a consistent voice she could rely on.[2] The result? She became one of the greatest singers of the twentieth century.

You see, even a tremendously gifted artist like Birgit Nilsson struggled. She had difficult days when she didn't know if she could develop enough technique to carry her through a career, when she didn't have money and had to borrow dresses for performances. She had to work hard. She had to stay focused.

You also have a "diamond" in your throat. And just as a diamond is formed deep in the earth, laboriously mined, cut, polished, and finally placed in a well-crafted setting so it can shine in all its glory, your voice is formed deep in the core of your being through an intense process of biomechanics, acoustics, cognition, and emotions.

Becoming a great singer isn't about your "gift." It isn't about being "good enough." Becoming a great singer means discovering how to align your thoughts, emotions, and behavior to tell the story of the music and lyrics, no matter what you sing.

Performing for an audience can be transformative. Whether singing for family and friends, on the stage of the Met, or in Madison Square Garden, sharing and expressing your message will take you to an extraordinary place. You have everything you need to get there. You only have to *craft* your diamond, "remove the carbon" until you have a powerful, flexible, and expressive instrument.

In the following chapters, you'll learn and practice training methods developed by master teachers of the past five centuries. The exercises in this book have trained Grammy winners, Broadway stars, and opera singers, as well as students and recreational singers of all ages. Thousands of singers have depended on these exercises and this approach to train the coordination of their voices.

Before you begin training, you need to prepare—just as you would prepare for running a marathon. Singing is more complex than most sports, so you'll need to prepare your voice, mind, and body.

◆ ◆ ◆

Singing creates a whirlwind of physical and emotional experiences for singers and listeners. While we luxuriate in a flurry of vibrations, airflow, memory, imagination, and sound, we tend to forget that singing is a motor skill, like riding a bicycle or using chopsticks. Learning a physical action, a motor skill, is called motor learning. Understanding the principles of motor learning can help you train your voice quickly and efficiently.

When you learn to ride a bicycle, you get basic instructions about the bike and where to put your hands and feet. You learn where the brakes and the gears are located, and then you swing your leg over the frame, hop on the seat, and push the pedals down to propel the bicycle forward. If no one is holding the bike when you pedal the first time, the bike will tip to one side or you'll fall. But as you pedal the bike with someone holding it, your skin, muscles, ligaments, and bones feel the forces of gravity, the weight of the bicycle, and the road beneath the bicycle. The body sends that information to your brain. As soon as your brain begins receiving information, it begins sending messages back to your body to correct your body position—tensing the right muscles, relaxing others, adjusting every aspect of your body required to balance on the bike. While you're enjoying the view and feeling the breeze on your face, your neurological system feverishly collects and sends messages throughout your brain and body in the background of your mind. You're not even aware of the activity that's going on because its unconscious, but you gradually feel the results. With each pedal, messages get faster and faster until the movement becomes automatic. Suddenly, your mother or father or sister or brother lets go, and you have your first taste of freedom, flying down the road with the wind in your hair.

Learning to sing is very similar. While you're singing, your mind is gathering sensory information, forming connections, storing the connections, and finally moving them to long-term memory until the movements become automatic and you can sing with the same freedom as flying down a hill on a bicycle. Singing involves incredibly complex movements: posture and respiration; coordination of the muscles inside the larynx, mouth, lips, tongue, throat, face, and jaw; and synchronicity with our amazing auditory system. You have to *allow* the unconscious neurological activity to take place. You can do that by focusing on sensory information—that is, your *experience* while singing.[3]

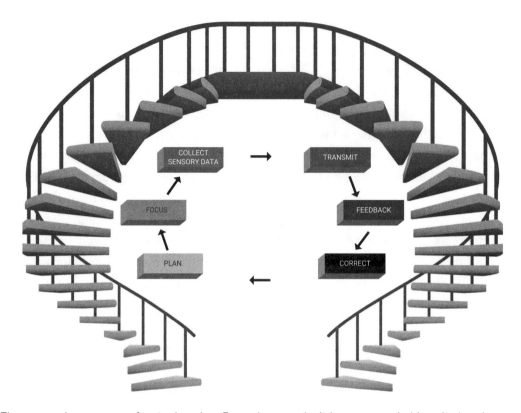

The unconscious process of motor learning. Even when you don't know, your mind is quite busy!

You don't learn to balance on a bicycle by thinking about how fast you'd like to ride, which hill you'd like to explore, or the feeling of your feet on the pedals. You have to focus on the feeling of balance. It would take a very long time to learn how to balance on a bicycle if you weren't directing your attention to the feeling of the bike, the forces of gravity, and the weight of your body. When someone is holding the bicycle for you, it easy for you to relax and allow your sensory system to collect the information it needs. The same is true for learning how to sing. You don't learn to sing effortlessly by thinking about "hit-

ting" the high notes, getting a "beautiful" sound, or how your throat feels. In singing, you have to focus on the senses of hearing, seeing, and physical sensation. In this book, these focus skills are called *tactilize*, *audicize*, and *visualize*.

Tactilize means directing your attention to the memory of a physical sensation. Do you remember the feeling of a dog's fur? Have you kneaded dough to make bread? Can you recall the feeling of the dough giving in to your hands? If you play tennis or dance, you have to remember the feeling of the body movements and positions in space. When you listen to or play music, you feel the beat, either viscerally or in actual movement, like tapping your foot.[4] When singing, you can learn to feel resonance, vibrato, lung pressure, a relaxed larynx, or the feeling of "compression" or "leaning in" you'll need to sing powerfully. There is a "touch" that singers sense at the start of a tone. The manner in which you "touch" is dictated by the music and style, and this feeling can be memorized. When you direct your attention toward physical sensations that occur effortlessly, you'll learn faster and more efficiently. All singers use the sense of physical feeling and touch to sing.

Audicize means directing your attention toward your memory of a sound. You can "hold" the sound in your mind. (Sometimes it's difficult to get the music in your mind to stop so you can get some sleep!) You can audicize the sound of vowels, tone, or memories of melody and harmony. Can you recall the sound of your mother's voice? What does your favorite animal's voice sound like? Can you remember the vocal tone of your favorite singer? Can you hear in your mind the last time you sang a great high note? Every singer uses sound sense, and memory of a sound to sing. Our memory of sound and voice is so powerful it can be a problem; if you've been listening to one singer for a long time, the sound of that voice can take over your hearing. You may have to train your mind to hear the sound of your own voice instead. You can also train your hearing to recognize vow-els and the acoustic properties of the tone (harmonics, frequencies, and amplitude).

Visualize means directing your attention toward your memory or idea of the way things look. Even blind people and animals have a "visual" memory. The visual cortex of their brains show activity when they remember an object or a position. They may not see the color and full details, but they remember the shape and spatial aspects of things they've experienced. So everyone has visual memory. Do you remember where you were last Sunday afternoon? Picture the place in your mind. Can you recall the colors, the shapes, the lighting? Can you see it in your mind's eye? That's visualizing, and you can use this skill to sing more effortlessly, freely, and expressively. You can visualize yourself singing onstage if you want to prepare for a performance—imagine the position of your mouth while singing a great *oo* vowel or standing with great posture. Visualizing is a sense that every singer uses to sing. You can learn to use it intentionally so that you can master your singing and performing.

Singers use all these senses when they sing. You can learn to direct your attention so you can change ineffective habits, develop better coordination in your voice, sing with more power and range, and be more expressive with the words and music. In the upcoming exercises and practice sessions, we're going to learn how to apply this to your singing until it becomes effortless.

TACTILIZE

AUDICIZE

VISUALIZE

◆ ◆ ◆

Singing involves many sections of the brain: areas responsible for thinking, hearing, feeling, movement of a variety of muscles, ligments, and bones. Neuroscience has discovered that the *connections between sections* of the brain have the most impact on how we function. Learning means using information from your experience to change and form these connections. This is called neuroplasticity. You're able to change and learn new things because your brain is "moldable." That's what you're doing when you're learning to ride a bicycle or learning to sing—you're molding connections that will make it possible for you to sing with freedom, power, and flexibility. While learning, the volume of your brain actually increases!

If you want to change your singing, you have to change your focus.

Once the new connections are firmly established, the volume returns to its previous size. Our brain is so *smart*; you just have to *allow* this to happen. If you're distracted by your voice, your sound, or your fears and beliefs, the unconscious functions of the brain don't work very well.[5]

You can create the best environment for motor learning by focusing on your senses. Focus means directing your attention. You're continuously directing your attention, either consciously or unconsciously. You focus when you brush your teeth, although it's so automatic that you're only aware of focusing for a nanosecond, while your unconscious mind is quite busy carrying out all the signaling that needs to take place to get the toothbrush between all the nooks and crannies. When you're learning something new, you need to consciously focus much more and for a longer time because you're forming new neural networks.[6]

Where do you direct your attention when you're singing, intentionally or unintentionally? You've seen that your brain collects a great deal of sensory information when you're learning, working feverishly to develop new connections. The information it collects depends on where you're directing your attention, your focus. If you're thinking about whether or not you sound good, or what other people think of your voice, or what you ate for breakfast, you won't be learning how to sing, or delivering your best performance. If you're directing your attention toward negative or limiting beliefs—" I don't think I can do this," "I don't understand this," "My voice can't sing that high"—repeatedly reaching for high notes or blowing huge amounts of air to get through challenging areas, you won't be singing with freedom, power, and flexibility. Focusing on the past or future, or on negative thoughts, is *unintentional*. Good singers are very *intentional*. They direct their attention to the sensory information they need to sing easily and expressively.

You will learn more about this later, but for now, remember it's important to *write down your experiences and perceptions* so you can find out where you're focusing and how to change it. Developing intentional focus will allow you to grow the neural connections you need to master the craft of singing.

So, now you know. No matter your "talent," no matter your singing ability now, no matter what problems you may have had in the past or with other voice training, no matter how many years you've been struggling, you can learn to sing freely and effectively.

◆ ◆ ◆

Words to Help You Focus on Your Experience

- *Tactilize* means focusing your attention on your physical sensations so you can memorize the *physical sensation*, or "touch," of what you're going to sing *before* you sing it.

- *Audicize* means using your mind's ear to memorize what you've heard and hold it in your mind, especially *before* you sing, but also for feedback while singing.

- *Visualize* means using your mind's eye to see what you want *before* you do it.

Throughout this book, you'll find questions, troubleshooting, and reflections to help you chart your experiences, fine-tune your craft, and build your understanding of your own experiences. At first, they may seem time consuming, or like *extra* work, but these tools are *crucial*: they will help you form neural connections stronger and faster than you ever thought possible. And you'll continue discovering more and more when you can look back on your answers throughout your training, even for the rest of your life. As you progress, answering will become easier, helping you to facet your voice, until knowing becomes a simple habit.

1.1 ZERO IN

When singers come to me for the first training session, I need to know a few specific things about them before I listen to their voice. I have to consider conditions that could be affecting their voice or I may not understand what I'm hearing. If you sang a big concert the night before, or if you have a chronic cough, the sound of your voice may be different than if you just came back from holiday. When I understand your current conditions, I can evaluate your singing more effectively and choose exercises that work for you in the specific moment.

Now this is *your* job. Before you begin training your voice, you can evaluate the current condition of your voice and singing habits. When you answer the following questions, you'll understand a great deal about conditions that are affecting the way you sing.

Circle the best answer for your current conditions.

1. Do you feel hoarse or "tired" in your throat today?

    Yes / No

2. Do you warm-up or balance your voice before singing?

    Yes / No

3. How much time do you spend everyday training your voice?

    A) None.   B) A few minutes.   C) An hour.   D) Whatever I need.

4. Does your voice get tired when you're learning new repertoire, memorizing a song, or writing a song?

    Yes / No

5. How is your general health? Do you have any current health conditions that may be affecting your voice? Asthma, allergies, sinus issues, respiratory ailments, metabolic issues, history of nodes, muscle tension dysphonia?

    A) My health is great.   B) I have a health issue.   C) I have a history of vocal issues.

Answer key

1. **No.** Congratulations. Now ask yourself this question everyday so you can memorize the sensation and *tactilize*.
    Yes. Uh-oh. Do you know why?

2. **Yes.** Congratulations! Now, does it help? Do you sing better this way? Are you directing your intention during your warm up?
   No. Uh-oh. Time to reevaluate. Can you *audicize* what you want from your voice?

3. D is the right answer: *whatever you need.* If you practice too quickly, maybe you are not being intentional. If you practice too long, maybe you're not using the right tools, or you need to develop a calm mental focus. Can you *visualize* a great practice session? What would have to happen to make a practice *great* for you?

4. **No.** Congratulations! You're doing great, but maybe you want to zero in on your energy levels. Are you using energy and intensity in your practice, like you must do in performance?
   Yes. Uh-oh. You're reinforcing neural networks that will be ineffective for effortless singing. Can you *visualize* your performance? Can your *audicize* your music and songs? Can you *tactilize*—feel the resonance and the sensation of a balanced voice?

5. Consider how your general health or past health issues may be affecting your singing today. Respiratory conditions, hormonal changes, anxiety and stress, attention challenges, allergies, acid reflux and many other health conditions affect your voice too. You can develop strategies to manage any conditions you face. Take stock of conditions now so you can manage them more effectively as you gain experience. But, keep in mind, if you feel your throat has been uncomfortable, with loss of tone or range for more than two weeks, seek the advice of a laryngologist who has experience with singers.

Zeroing in on the general condition of your voice is an important habit. As a singer, or anyone using their voice for speaking or singing on a regular basis, you're usually multitasking. You may be in school, at work, writing and rehearsing, or living in a place with capricious weather. Or you're on tour, sleeping in hotels and on buses, eating catering or restaurant food. All these conditions affect your singing. You may not notice that your voice is getting a little tired. Maybe you're nursing sinus congestion, or so tired that you have to just push through. If you aren't in the habit of zeroing in on the condition of your voice and using strategies to respond, you'll suddenly find yourself struggling to sing in your typical range, or losing power and intonation.

1.2 GEAR UP

There are a few tools you can use to make learning more fun and more effective. Check out this list and think about the best tools for you. Do you have what you need to successfully learn from this book? If not, start with whatever you have, and add what you need as you go through the training.

Answer yes or no.

_____ Do you have a device you can use to take photos and video of your singing (smart-phone, computer, camera)?

_____ Will you be singing with the online recordings (www.lindaballiro.com)?

_____ If so, do you have a speaker on your device that's loud enough to hear while you're singing? If you can't hear the music, you'll sing too quietly, if the music is blasting, you may push too much.

_____ Will you be playing the scales on a keyboard or piano? There are online keyboards, apps and inexpensive keyboards you can attach to your computer if you don't have your own keyboard/piano.

_____ Do you have a peaceful place where you can study and practice?

_____ Do you have a notebook or a file on your device where you can write your answers and questions?

_____ Do you have a music stand or a high table/desk where you can put the book and/or your music?

_____ Do you have a metronome? Singers can't hear a metronome while singing but there are metronome apps that have lights.

_____ Do you have a pencil, pen, or marker so you can write answers and highlight this book or your music?

_____ Do you have a buddy who can support you on this journey? A friend, colleague, family member?

Gather the best tools for your own situation. You know best which of the tools you'll need. You may not be able to decide right away, so after you start training, you can come back to this list for ideas or changes to your plan. Singing and voice training enriches your life in many ways, but it can also be hard work, so preparing your tools before using the training materials in this book, and having a friend, family member, singer or teacher you can call to support your efforts, may make it easier and more fun.

1.3 FOCUS

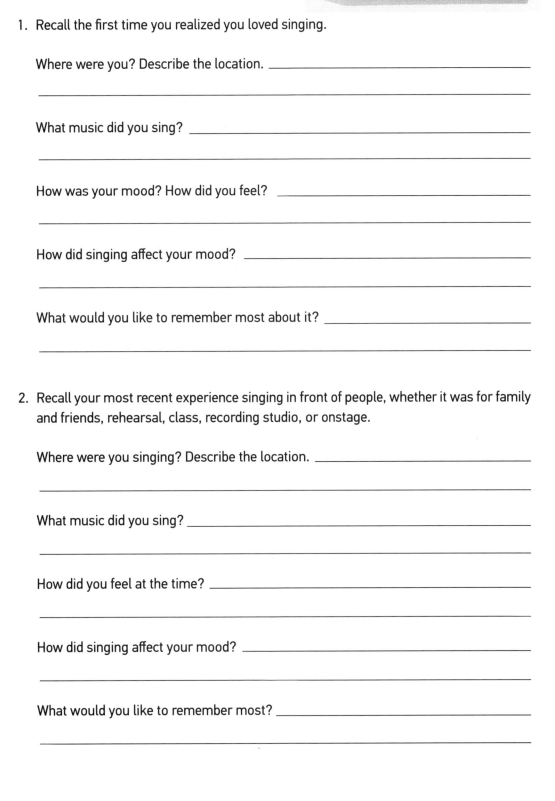

1. Recall the first time you realized you loved singing.

   Where were you? Describe the location. _____
   _____

   What music did you sing? _____
   _____

   How was your mood? How did you feel? _____
   _____

   How did singing affect your mood? _____
   _____

   What would you like to remember most about it? _____
   _____

2. Recall your most recent experience singing in front of people, whether it was for family and friends, rehearsal, class, recording studio, or onstage.

   Where were you singing? Describe the location. _____
   _____

   What music did you sing? _____
   _____

   How did you feel at the time? _____
   _____

   How did singing affect your mood? _____
   _____

   What would you like to remember most? _____
   _____

What would you like to change for the next time? _____

_____

3. Imagine the next time you will be singing in front of people, whether for family and friends, rehearsal, class, recording studio, or onstage.

Where would you want to be singing? Describe the location. _____

_____

What would you want to sing? _____

_____

How would you like to feel when you're singing? How would you like your singing to affect you and your listeners? _____

_____

FINAL CHECK

You can take a few moments now to look through the previous material and be sure that you have everything you need to be comfortable and confident about moving ahead. WARNING: Read this book and do the exercises in order, without skipping around, regardless of how much experience you have. If you are an experienced singer, you may be able to go through them quickly, but if you are a new singer, you may need a few weeks on each series of scales, maybe taking two to four months to go through the whole training. After you've been through the training, you should be able to use the book as a reference and skip around to the exercises that work best for you.

2

DISCOVER *WHAT* NEEDS TRAINING

The key is to begin with the end in mind. You're always imagining,
"What's going to come out of this? What's in there?"

—Chandra Horn, academic director for Canada's Montreal School of Gemology[1]

In the last chapter, you discovered your diamond, and you prepared to become an intentional singer by zeroing in on conditions and learning about focusing on your senses by *tactilizing*, *audicizing*, and *visualizing*. Now, let's dig deeper and show you that knowing how your voice functions *now* will lead to masterful singing *later*.

When a diamond is unearthed, it's called a rough diamond. It's straight from the soil, untouched by human hands. Each diamond has "inclusions"—little pieces of the universe embedded deep in the stone—that create reflections and affect its clarity and color.

 TACTILIZE

 AUDICIZE

 VISUALIZE

These imperfections can add beauty to the stone, but they also show areas of stress and strain, just like voices.

When rough diamonds are evaluated, all the inclusions are measured and examined, so the gemologist can decide how to cut it. Could it be a round cut for an engagement ring? Is a triangle cut the only possibility? If so, how would it be used? The gemologist creates a vision of how to cut the stone based on these inclusions. Some inclusions, or *flaws*, make the rough diamond worthless, while others just determine the style and shape the diamond can become and can even increase its value. One has to "begin with the end in mind." A master lapidary artist can transform a rough diamond with flaws into a beautiful work of art for jewelry or any other setting.

> **"Pockets of stress areas and strain can lead to the stone literally exploding and/or shattering while we are trying to saw it, polish it or place a facet on it."**
>
> **—Chandra Horn[2]**

When singers come to me to develop their voice, I have to *visualize* and *audicize* what each singer can become. I have to listen for their unique characteristics so I can evaluate the conditions of the voice, body, and mind of the singer. This is the only way I can determine which training must follow. Just as the lapidary artist asks herself how to cut the rough diamond, I ask myself, "How will I be able to help this singer become who he or she wants to be?" More important, how can I teach this singer to polish or facet his or her voice? What intentions should this singer develop? How much experience does this singer have with motor learning? Now you can ask *yourself* the same kind of questions so you can develop your ability to tactilize, audicize, and visualize. Can you begin with the end in mind? Can you find out what your voice can become?

2.1 SCALE SERIES
Assess with a Five-Tone Scale

FIVE-TONE SCALE ASSESSMENT

In the following exercise, you'll sing a short scale to evaluate your own singing habits. You'll use the same criteria I use in private lessons. This scale will show you where you have "inclusions"—areas of stress and strain. This scale is your tool to find out how your voice functions now. Don't worry if you can't sing all the notes or if you aren't used to singing in this range, just sing and find out what happens. Then you'll have information to help you train your voice with the scales that follow.

1. Choose the scale for your voice type.

2. Play the scale on piano or listen to the audio file, <u>even if you know the scale.</u>

3. Say the vowel *uh*, like the English word *fun* (IPA=ʌ).[3] Can you audicize the vowel before you sing?

4. Feel the rhythm! Tap your foot to the beat. Relax your hands.

5. Sing a cappella, or while playing piano or audio file.

6. Sing only as low or as high as you feel comfortable. You don't need to sing all the notes in the examples.

7. When you're finished, write down the answers to the following questions.
   (Remember we're writing things down to form faster and stronger neural connections.)

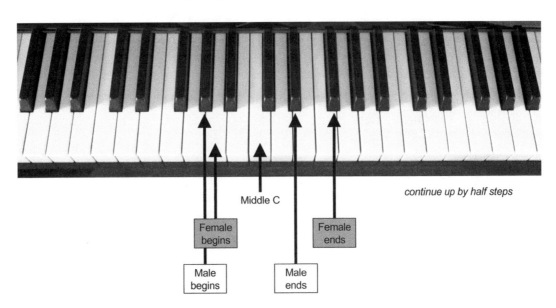

Middle C

continue up by half steps

Female begins

Female ends

Male begins

Male ends

A. Mark on the notation or keyboard photo where you stopped singing the scale.

B. Why did you stop singing?

C. Answer these questions:

Vowel. Was the *uh* clear?

1. I think so.
2. No, it sounded like yelling.
3. It changed a few times while I was singing.
4. I don't know.

Dynamics. How loud or soft were you, and did that change?

1. My singing was loud.
2. My singing was soft.
3. I got louder as the pitch went up.
4. The top was louder than the bottom.
5. The bottom was louder than the top.
6. I don't know.

Tone clarity. What was the tone quality of your singing?
1. The tone was clear.
2. The tone was noisy.
3. The tone was breathy.
4. I don't know.

Resonance. How resonant did your singing feel to you?
1. I felt resonance on the bottom but not on the top.
2. I felt resonance on the top but not on the bottom.
3. I didn't feel any resonance.
4. I don't know.

Vibrato. Was there any vibrato? If so, what was it like?
1. There wasn't any vibrato.
2. The vibrato was wide.
3. The vibrato was uneven.
4. The vibrato was fast and shaky.
5. I don't know.

Intonation. Were you in tune the whole time?
1. The pitches were clear and even.
2. The pitches began clear but changed during the scale.
3. I think so.
4. I don't know.

What did you experience?
1. I couldn't control it.
2. My throat felt tight.
3. It felt airy.
4. The feeling changed during the exercise.

Now, turn on your audio or video recorder and record yourself singing the scale again.

When you're finished, listen to the recording and answer the questions again. (Yes! Answer the questions a second time. You may have different answers because you're already learning.)

DEBRIEF

This scale is a tool for discovering how your singing functions now. You want to find out the answers to these questions:

o How does your voice move from lower to higher notes?

o How much can you affect what's happening when you sing?

o Are there things about the sound or feeling that you don't like?

The answers to the above questions can show you what you need to train in the coming chapters.

◆ If you answered "I don't know" to many of these questions, don't worry. You will find answers in the next scales.

◆ If you were able to change your answers the second time, congratulations! That shows you were able to increase your sensory awareness just by answering the questions— getting the plan in your mind so you could focus!

◆ If you wanted to sing differently the second time, but you couldn't do it, that's great too, because that shows you the areas where you can improve your singing.

Right now, you're discovering *where* you need to train your voice. Which part of your voice isn't easy and effortless? Can your voice move along the scale without reaching, losing tone quality, or feeling uncomfortable? *The place in the scale where your tone changes suddenly, where you feel uncomfortable, or where you can't move easily, is the area you need to train.* This may be different than your past experience—if you're preparing for a concert, or an audition, you certainly don't want to focus on the part of your voice that doesn't work the easiest or sound the best. But that's exactly what you need to focus on in this training. You need to find the trouble spots and apply the tools you're learning to resolve them. There shouldn't be any "trouble spots" or stress areas in your voice. You have to *eliminate* the stress areas because they are having a negative impact on your *entire* voice and everything you sing. My students and clients do it, and so can you.

◆ ◆ ◆

Sometimes voice training is difficult. You have to work hard to change habits in your mind and body because singing is a complex skill. When we sing, we're expressing our thoughts and feelings, like telling a story, and we're using a complex motor system that engages a great deal of neurological activity. Each experience we have informs our neural system, a moldable network of connections that make it possible for us to function. For example, each time you pull or reach for a note, or blow a lot of air, you're training your neural pathways—in the wrong path. That's why you need to direct your attention to the things that will help you improve. Develop intentional focus. We will discuss each aspect of how to do this in coming chapters, but you can begin now by taking the time to engage your voice, mind, and body as you would in "real-world" singing. If you try out these exercises when you're sitting on the sofa with your feet up, or making dinner while "taking a look at" the exercises, you won't get any benefit. Success depends on *where* and *how* you direct your attention. Directing your attention requires "readiness"—physical commitment to begin an action, like a runner crouching at the starting line of a race. Approach the exercises as you would a private lesson with your dream coach, or better yet, a dream performance. Even though the exercises may be short, odd, silly, or difficult, you will get the most benefit when you perform them for "real," not just "trying them out." And writing and recording your experiences will make it easier to focus, observe, and *stay in the moment* so you don't have to listen and analyze while you're singing. Just sing. Allow the exercises and the evaluations to give you the *experience* you need to make changes. And one more thing: don't forget to *have fun.*

Though we're just getting started, you've done some important learning already. You've identified where your voice doesn't easily move, or where you lose tone quality, or where something doesn't happen the way you wanted. Maybe you haven't been able to find out exactly what's going on, but you'll discover more each time you use a scale. You can also understand by reading the following examples of singers doing the same exercise in their first voice lesson. Which one of the following coaching sessions sounds like you?

LINDA: First, I'm just going to hear you sing so I can find out about your voice and how you sing. We're not training anything yet. I'm just going to listen to you sing. After the exercise, we'll talk about what happened and make a plan based on that, OK?

YOU: Sounds great.

LINDA: (*Sings and plays a five-tone scale on piano.*) We'll just go up by half steps like this, as long as you're comfortable, OK?

YOU: OK.

LINDA: (*Plays five-tone scale and singer sings along with piano.*)

BEGINNER EXAMPLE: FEMALE

LINDA: (*Stops playing at F4.*) OK, great, thank you. I know you can sing much higher than this, but we can stop there because I have enough information to make a plan for you right now. I hear that you started off singing the lower part well—nice voice, sounded solid, but as we got to around here (*plays G4–A4–B-flat4*), things changed. I couldn't understand the vowel anymore, and you were reaching for the pitches. Not so comfortable?

You: I know what you mean.

Linda: Is this typically what happens when you sing?

You: Yes, most of the time, I don't know what to do there and it's uncomfortable. I don't like the sound.

Linda: OK, no worries. Most singers have to learn how to do that. You don't have a problem with range, just with the transition from low to high—there's a "bridge"—some people call this a break or a passaggio. Singers need to learn to go through there without changing the vowel or the tone quality, because many songs have their chorus or power sections in this range. If you can move around in this area of your voice like you are talking, you'll have many choices available when you sing songs. Does that make sense?

You: Am I supposed to be singing that area in chest voice?

Linda: Chest voice is just another word for your talking voice. It's the part of your voice where you usually speak. Many people use words like chest and head voice to describe sound, but you will find it easier to think about these words as describing a *function*. Learn how the different areas of your voice behave and where you can focus to improve them.

You: So when do I switch to head voice?

Linda: You shouldn't have to switch anything—our voice is an amazing system that is capable of complex sounds and movements. You can feel the change in airflow, or resonance, as you change range, but that is just vibrations caused by the sound waves coming out your mouth. You shouldn't feel any "switching" in your throat or voice. Let's start with finding your upper voice, or head voice, so you can begin hearing and feeling what it's like to be solid in that part of your voice.

DEBRIEF

This singer was "reaching" for the notes as she moved through her range. Do you think you're singing like this? If you feel like you're lifting your head up during the scale, or using a lot of muscles in your neck, and your vowel changes to *ah*, like the word *father*, you may be reaching. *Ah* tends to be more difficult to sing for many people, and it can indicate that you're losing control of intonation and dynamics. Right now, *uh* is easier to sing, so if you feel like you're reaching for the notes like this singer did, audicize the *uh* before you sing. Can you hear the vowel in your mind and hold it in your mind *while* you're singing? Can you keep the volume even, so you don't sing louder as you go through the scale? You may want to start training your voice by exploring the upper notes.

Can you tactilize how you should begin the tone? Is your "touch" at the start of the tone too firm or too light?

BEGINNER EXAMPLE: MALE

LINDA: (*Stops playing at a E-flat4.*) OK, great, so you started off with a nice, solid voice. I know you can sing much higher than this, but I stopped here because you lost your connection. The tone changed a lot. . . . It got very quiet, like a falsetto.

YOU: Yes, sorry. I can get louder there sometimes, but I didn't want to push. Not sure what to do there.

LINDA: No worries. Most people have to train to be able to sing that well, and most male voices have trouble with this area (*plays E4–F4–F-sharp4*). So sometimes you can sing with a solid tone there?

YOU: I can do it in songs, but it doesn't sound good, and it feels really uncomfortable.

LINDA: That's what happens if you try to force your way through—it's the area where the voice is changing from low to high. It's challenging to find out how to go through there and stay in a "talking" voice. So we don't lose the tone quality or feel really uncomfortable. Yelling doesn't sound very good, and anyone can yell! But singing breathy, or falsetto, to avoid yelling doesn't help either!

YOU: I don't want to push, but I don't know how to make it sound stronger.

LINDA: It's tricky! If you think about it more as coordination rather than strength, you will get better results. The feeling we have when singing is usually a lot different than we expect it to be. We hear professional singers "belting" pop songs, and opera singers with rich, ringing tones, and it makes us think of strength. But actually, when your singing sounds strong, it feels light and easy. Of course, singing with energy is always a cardio workout, but it's never a workout here (*points to throat*). To keep your *tone solid* as you go through this range, so you don't lose tone quality, you have to discover how to stay in contact. It's a physical sensation of making contact at the start of the tone in just the right amount, along with feeling vibrations and moving air. Let's try developing your contact in the upper part of your voice.

DEBRIEF

Does this sound familiar to you? I call it the *Goldilocks syndrome*—not too hot and not too cold, just right. Many singers face this challenge: how to sing throughout your range without yelling (too loud to control intonation or dynamics) or getting breathy/falsetto (too quiet to control intonation and tone quality). Keeping the vowel *consistent*—without changing from *uh* to *ah*—is the first step to develop the ability to move easily from low to high. Eventually, of course you can sing any vowel you want, but right now, some vowels help you more than others, so use them! (Don't worry! We're going to practice this a lot so you'll become a master at singing vowels.) NOTE: If you feel like the lower part of your voice is pretty reliable, or you are a singer who sings in your low voice most of the time, you can dive right in to the triad scale in chapter 3. You may get faster results if you skip the low exercises for now. You can come back to check in on them after you've found your upper voice.

INTERMEDIATE/ADVANCED EXAMPLE: FEMALE

LINDA: OK, nice job. I know you can sing much higher, but we can stop there for now. I hear that you have a great voice and you go through your first bridge, or transition, in the octave above middle C pretty well, but as we approach the second bridge in the next octave (F5–A-flat 5), you were driving a lot of air to push through. You have a good voice, so it still sounds pretty good, but it's not quite in the center of the pitch, and the tone quality isn't as nice as I know you have. Does that make sense?

YOU: You mean, at the passaggio?

LINDA: Yes, you will find it easiest to think of this area as your second passaggio, or bridge, because most women feel a change in resonance here (*plays first bridge*) and here (*plays second bridge*). A great deal of opera and art song spends time around this range, and even though those notes are natural for your voice, you can learn to sing them with much less effort—then the middle of your voice will also develop more color and flexibility. So if you're singing contemporary music, you'll get more power in your voice if this second bridge is easier. It's *a little* like how runners or other athletes get more power and flexibility by stretching out their hamstrings.

YOU: I don't really feel like I'm using a lot of effort in my throat.

LINDA: Sometimes we can't feel it at first because we're blowing a lot of air. So while you're singing, you may not feel a lot of muscle, but when you stop singing, you will notice a feeling of tiredness or hoarseness. You may feel like you have trouble getting back down to lower notes after you sing that range with too much effort, or you may feel you're not exactly in the center of the pitch, which was happening just now. Does that make sense?

YOU: I think so. My voice does feel tired sometimes, and everyone keeps telling me I need to support more.

LINDA: Support is part of the picture, but you'll find your voice works more efficiently and with less effort when you develop better coordination. It sounds like you've been singing by tanking up on air, taking bigger breaths than you need. The voice is actually performing some complex little movements when we're moving through different ranges, and we have to allow that to happen. If we over-breathe, with too much effort for the inhale, we will actually inhibit that coordination. Like learning to ride a bicycle, when you find the right balance, your voice will just work. Then you can engage more support, controlling the exhale, depending on the style of music you're singing. Let's try another exercise so you feel what it's like to go through that range with less effort and more clarity.

DEBRIEF

If you've been singing for a while, maybe after years of voice training and performing, you may recognize yourself in this example. The singer moves much higher in her range without any noticeable problems, but at the second bridge, the second place where the voice transitions from low to high, some problems start to show. Singers with great voices can hide things behind a big breath. Many classical singers inhale too much air with too much effort. If the voice can naturally make a big sound, the singer may sound impressive at first, but without the proper coordination in the voice, problems start to show, and the singer always feels like something isn't right. The solution is the same as in the above examples: finding more contact in your voice so you have coordination, rather than large amounts of air. It's difficult to know at first what's causing the lack of coordination. You will have to start with exploring the basics of your voice to find out if you've been "hiding" any tensions.

Which coaching session sounded like you? Can you guess when the singer is *tactilizing, audicizing,* or *visualizing*? How could you tactilize, audicize, or visualize to master your singing?

Following are examples of the areas where most people have inconsistencies in their voices. These are general guidelines. It's impossible to write "rules" for your voice because you are unique. But you can use these guidelines to discover the areas of your voice where you lose tone quality, intonation, vowel clarity, or the ability to sing at all dynamic levels. These are often called bridges, transitions, passaggi, or breaks, but it's easiest for you to begin thinking about your voice as one instrument with a few areas where you need tools or strategies to make things easier, develop the tone you want, and have more choices about what to sing. The guides show a range, but you may only feel like one or two notes within that range don't work for you, or you may find you can't get past the first one! Use the training to find your answers. Remember, your own experience will teach you. If you can't find out which guide is the closest to your voice, choose the best one for now. You can change your mind later if you need to.

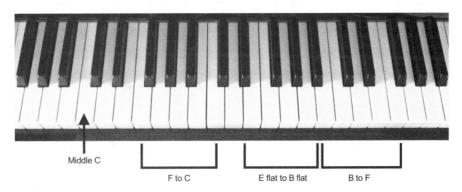

If you have a higher female voice, you may find this guide helpful to find areas where your voice loses tone quality, feels uncomfortable, or doesn't sound in tune. You may be able to sing higher than this.

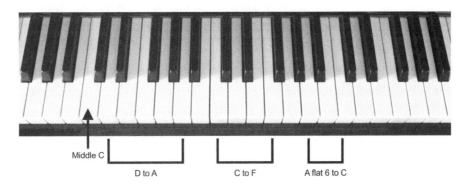

If you have a lower female voice, you may recognize changes in your voice here.

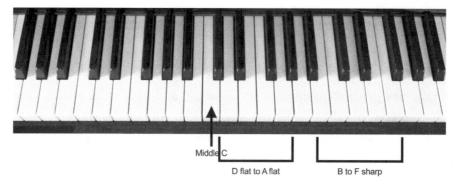

Middle C

D flat to A flat   B to F sharp

Higher male voices may recognize these transitions. But you may sing much higher than this too!

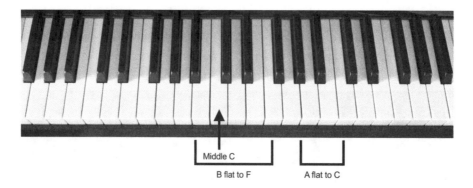

Middle C

B flat to F   A flat to C

Lower male voices usually have to train these areas. You may sing much lower than this. What about soprano, mezzo, alto, tenor, bass, and the other voice types? Types are important for singing in a choir, choosing musical theater roles, or building art song/opera repertoire. But, many singers are told their "type" before the voice is ready, causing problems as the voice evolves. You'll save time if you first train to easily move from lower to upper voice with a range of dynamics. Then the strengths of your voice will unearthed, making it easy to choose roles and repertoire that are best for your type.

In the lessons above, there was a lot of language used to describe sounds of the voice. Chest, head, mix, break . . . the list of terms goes on and on. While words may be helpful to understand concepts, using words to describe sounds and sensations can be confusing or inadequate. I've met many singers who have been completely confused by trying to figure out all these words, searching for some elusive, mysterious vocal acrobatics they're "supposed to be" doing. Over time, the words just get longer and more mysterious. It takes serious study to try to understand what these words actually mean.

Using words to describe sound and sensation grew from the early days of vocal pedagogy, in the Schola Cantorum, the Italian singing school that dominated singing in the Middle Ages. Small groups of men and boys chanting sustained melodic lines with liturgical texts demanded consistent resonance and perfect legato (smooth, connected) singing. It took the students nine years to master their singing technique. Without any medical science or research to show them the way, students of the Schola Cantorum were taught with the language of personal experience—low notes sung with resonance cause the singer to feel a lot of vibration in the mouth and chest ("chest" voice) while singing higher notes with resonance cause the singer to feel a lot of vibration in the face, nose, between the ears ("head" voice.) "Mix" referred to singing in one smooth movement, so the difference between upper and lower voice doesn't disrupt the sound. Sensations of resonance from the upper voice are connected to the lower voice when needed and sensations of the lower voice are connected to the upper voice when needed.[4] Shortly after the first treatise explaining vocal technique appeared, others followed with more words and opinions. By the early seventeenth century, there were dozens of opinions about how to train the voice and which words should be used to describe it.[5]

Today's music and singing expresses sounds from many historical and cultural influences, not just Europe. There's a wide range of tone qualities, resonance, and styles—even opera and art song, a form that originated from the great European composers, now encompass aspects of gospel, jazz, and roots music. Pop, jazz, rock, R&B and musical theater are music of the "new world" but are now completely international in scope and style, including musical influences from Africa, the Middle East, Asia, and South America. Singers from all countries incorporate music styles from Europe and America in their own languages, instruments, music history, and cultures. How can we find words to communicate the sounds and sensations of all these possibilities to help you become a better singer today?

These demands on singers require a paradigm shift. Words should help you define your experience while singing so you can refine your skills. Focus on simple concepts. Then, you can apply tools to create or enhance those experiences.

If you want to build a career in singing, you will have to become familiar with the language of that industry. For example, Broadway casting notices and directors ask for very specific voice types and skills, producers and recording engineers have vocabulary that they use in recoding sessions, and classical/opera conductors may use yet another set of words to ask for the sounds they want. You, as the singer, have to translate the words of the music industry to your own experience so you can show them what they want. When you have the skills, that's an easy task.

Here are words that can help you define your experience without adding mental clutter.

Lower voice: This is commonly called "chest." The singer may experience vibrations in the mouth and chest; well-produced lower notes may feel like your sternum is vibrating. Lower voice can be sung at all volumes and tone qualities—loud, quiet, breathy, firm, etc.

Upper voice: This is commonly called "head." The singer may experience vibrations in the face, behind the nose, and between, or in, the ears or head. Upper notes can be sung at all volumes and tone qualities. Falsetto is often used to describe upper notes that are very quiet and breathy.

Mix: Resonant singing at medium volume, like speaking, without unintended changes in tone quality. Vibrations can be felt and heard throughout the voice and the singing. The singer can also feel the changes in vibration moving from the mouth to the head, face, or nose area but doesn't feel anything changing or moving in the throat because the larynx is relaxed, as in speaking.

Light mix: Resonant singing at quiet or low volume. Singers still feel vibrations and airflow, and some engagement of the voice, but this is not falsetto, which is a change in tone quality as described above. The larynx is also relaxed, without "holding" or "squeezing" to control volume.

Strong mix: Resonant singing at a loud or high volume. Singers feel a great deal of vibration, usually in the face or head, and although very free from tension, they feel a comfortable compression in the voice. This is the power singing in contemporary pop, rock, R & B, and musical theater. The larynx is still generally relaxed but may be less so than in other kinds of singing.

◆ ◆ ◆

Semi-occluded vocal tract exercises (SOVT) such as singing through a straw or singing letters and sounds such as *v*, *m*, *n*, *ng*, lip rolls, tongue rolls, and, to some extent, *oo*, *ee* are an important tool.[6] SOVT exercises are like a gentle foot massage after you've been standing on your feet all day. Singers often use them to learn more about how to manage their voices, to warm up, to recover from a cold or cough, or to rehabilitate after over-singing. SOVT exercises allow you to feel vibrations in your face, lips, mouth, and nose so you can develop your ability to tactilize.

Semi-occluded means that the mouth is partially or fully closed (when the mouth is fully closed for *mm*, sound will exit through the nose). Although science now explains *why* SOVTs are helpful to singers and speakers, singers have reaped the rewards of singing "semi-occluded" for generations, if not hundreds of years—for example, vocal exercises on *oo*, *m*, *n*, or *ng* have been used by voice teachers and singers for a very long time. So why do they create such a cozy feeling for voices? How can they help you improve your singing?

The great benefit of SOVT exercises is that they reduce air pressure, so any muscle tension that may have built up when you've been yelling, reaching for high notes, or talking loud at a party, will also be reduced.[7]

There are a few more benefits to SOVT exercises. They will help you develop your sensory awareness of the four main processes that produce singing, speaking, or vocalizing (phonation).

Breathing: Lung pressure and airflow.

Pitch: Movement of the muscles of the larynx, the vocal folds, make the pitch we hear.

Intonation: Singing out of tune with the music or instruments is usually a result of tension and imbalance. SOVTs make it easier to improve intonation because of the reduced pressure.

The effect doesn't include blocking your mouth with unvoiced consonants like *s* or *f*. These consonants partially close your mouth, but they don't use your voice so they won't help you manage your singing. (If you're not sure what this means, put your finger on your Adam's apple and say *f* or *s*—then say *v* and *z*. When do you feel vibration?)

Aural feedback: SOVTs are smaller, focused sounds so you can develop your listening and hearing more easily than with full voice singing.

You can incorporate SOVT exercises into your daily life too—you can sing gliding sighs up and down through a straw or sing scales on a *vvv* throughout your day to keep your voice fresh and relaxed. Practice being aware of the sensations of vibrations in your lower and upper voice (Can you go low and high without reaching or pulling?), while staying relaxed in your mouth. You'll be improving your ability to tactilize and audicize for singing and keeping your voice in great shape.

COACHING TIP

When singing through a straw, or on another SOVT, the voice should move throughout the range, like a hum that moves easily up and down, not pushing volume, puffing out cheeks, or tensing the inside of your mouth. There should be no breaks in sound or puffs/hisses of air coming out through the straw or lips. Your stomach muscles should be loose, not squeezed or pulled in. The sound is something like a puppy whining for attention.

2.2 SCALE SERIES
Evaluate Intonation and Balance

FIVE-TONE SCALE ON LIP ROLLS

Lip rolls are bubbling with your lips while singing. Your mouth isn't open, you just vocalize while rolling your lips. This is a type of semi-occluded vocal tract exercise. It's a very fast way to relax your vocal folds. Many singers use them to warm up, recover from oversinging, and increase range.

1. Make fists with your hands. Place the flat part of your knuckles, the part you would use to punch something, on each side of your jaw below your mouth. Push the skin up, making your lips chubby and a little squished. Now, blow. Your lips should flutter. Have you seen babies blow their lips like this?

Can you audicize a dog's voice?

2. Keep your fists pushing up your lips and say *rum-tum-tum*. Before you sing, audicize the vowel *uh* (IPA= ʌ). Imagine a big, dopey dog. Your tongue should be lying flat in your mouth gently resting against your bottom front teeth.

3. Choose one note in a comfortable part of your voice, press your lips together a little, and sing with the pushed-up lips while audicizing *rum-tum-tum*. Your lips should flutter/bubble while you're singing.

4. Now sing the five-tone scale on the lip rolls.

    a. Choose the scale for your voice type.

    b. Play the scale on your instrument or listen to the audio file, <u>even if you know the scale.</u>

    c. Say *rum-tum-tum*. Can you audicize the vowel before you sing? Hold it in your mind.

    d. Sing a cappella, or while playing piano or audio file.

    e. Feel the rhythm! Tap your foot to the beat, relax your hands.

GOALS

Even though your lips are closed, you can audicize the vowel before and during singing. Maintain even volume, vowel, tone and lip rolls *throughout* the scale. This is consistency, and you need consistency to easily move in songs.

Sing this scale on lip rolls. Do you feel vibrations in your mouth? Audicize *uh*. Keep volume even. Avoid squeezing your stomach muscles while singing.

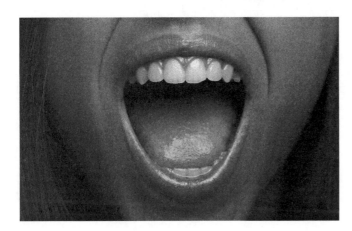

The tongue is complex! Can you relax yours like this? Then it can freely move while singing without pressing, pulling, or pushing.

Chart Your Experience

Answer yes, no, or don't know

AFTER SINGING   **AFTER RECORDING**

_____   I couldn't do the lip rolls.   _____

_____   I started the lip rolls, but I couldn't keep them going.   _____

_____   I had to push the air out really hard.   _____

_____   My throat felt tight.   _____

_____   The lip rolls stopped on the top note of the scale.   _____

_____   The lip rolls were even throughout the scale.   _____

No lip rolls | Lip rolls failed sometimes | Had to push air out | Lip rolls stopped on top notes | Lip rolls were even

DEBRIEF

If your lips don't roll:

o Is your tone consistent, or does it get quieter or louder during the scale?

o Are you inhaling too much, or blowing too hard when you sing?

o Are your lips loose and "chubby"?

COACHING TIP

How do you know if you're doing this scale effectively? You can check yourself:

- Push up your lips with your fists, but use the finger side of your fists to make your lips chubby, so you can also put your thumbs under your chin. That soft part under your chin is your tongue! While you're singing the lip rolls, that area under your chin should stay soft and not move at all during the scale. Can you feel it? Try singing the lip rolls and find out if your tongue moves or hardens. If it does, try singing very quietly until it doesn't move at all.

- Record yourself singing the scales on audio or video. Ask a buddy to watch or listen.

- Chart your experience again. Did any of your answers change?

- Finally, can you change the tempo (speed of the music)? Can you sing this scale very quickly?

These scales may seem simple at first, especially if you're an experienced singer, but they expose how your voice muscles are moving. If you're using your swallowing muscles when you sing, these exercises won't sound or feel easy; you won't be able to do them at a medium volume, or at different tempos. You will know there are issues because your *intonation* won't be accurate. Many singers are surprised when they try these simple scales and realize they aren't able to stay on the center of the pitch. This isn't a problem with your musical hearing but a problem with coordination—coordination of airflow/pressure, and muscles of the voice that make it possible for you to sing different pitches. Take your time with these scales and take notice: Are you really able to stay in tune? Are you on the center of the pitch? Can you manage the coordination that makes it possible to move quickly and easily through these areas of your voice without going "out of tune"?

2.3 SCALE SERIES
What's Happening in Your Lower Voice?

I. Although all areas of your voice must be developed to be in balance, the foundation for great singing begins in the lower voice. Many singers are quite comfortable singing in their low range, but others have trouble getting enough sound, or they unintentionally force/press on the lower notes. Do you know what happens when you sing the lower range? Every singer, classical or contemporary, needs to find out. Even classical sopranos need lower voices that are firm but comfortable because it's the basis for great high notes. Use the scales on pages 34–35 for this exercise.

- Practice saying *buh*, like the English word *butter* (IPA= bʌ). The *b* should be clear and easy, without pressing your lips too hard or puffing out your cheeks. Compare *b* and *p*. Can you feel the difference? They are the same consonant in your lips, but *b* is a voiced consonant. Your vocal folds vibrate when you say it. Make sure you're singing *b* and not *p*.

- Can you say the *buh* a little low and deep, like a big, dopey dog? The sound should feel like it's coming out your mouth, not your nose. Any sensations of vibration should be in your mouth or lower, not in the back of your mouth or behind your nose. Your jaw can go up and down a little, without pressing the inside of your mouth.

- When you've found the sensation in speaking, choose the scale in the most comfortable range for your voice. Sing only as low or high as you feel comfortable.

- Listen to the audio file, read or play the notation.

- Keep the tempo, feel the beat, and stay in the "mouthy," dopey dog voice for the entire exercise.

Chart Your Experience

Answer yes, no, or don't know.

AFTER SINGING   **AFTER RECORDING**

_____   Felt very light and sound was breathy.   _____

_____   Felt "thick" in my voice and sounded "flat."   _____

_____   My stomach was tight while singing.   _____

_____   Felt my throat going up with the pitch.   _____

_____   Vowel was clear and didn't change.   _____

_____   Felt easy and sounded "full."   _____

Very light and breathy | Felt "thick" | Stomach was tight | Vowel was clear | Felt easy

DEBRIEF

Singing on *buh* helps you relax your larynx so you can sing consistently without "shifting" anything. It also helps you balance the air and muscle, so you won't be pressing. The sound may be lower or deeper than you're used to, and it may even be louder. The feeling should be very open, loose, and easy.

COACHING TIP

If you don't feel any vibrations or sense of resonance, go back to speaking the *buh* until you feel confident.

Do you feel the airflow? Can your voice move quickly through the scale? Record yourself singing the scale and/or have your buddy watch you sing. You can watch the recording yourself or with your buddy.

What changed when you sang the second time? Do you feel open, easy, full sound coming out your mouth?

Use the 2.2 scale series one more time to increase the intensity without pressing or tension.

- Practice speaking *bagh*, like the English word *bat* (IPA= æ.) This sound is much uglier than *buh*. To find it, try cackling like a witch or a bratty child. Can you cackle comfortably, without squeezing or pressing?

- You will feel vibration toward the tip of your nose when you speak or sing, but you shouldn't feel thick in your throat or pressing in your mouth.

- Choose the scale that is most comfortable for you. You should be able to sing lower than you did before, even if you're a high voice. Only sing as long as you're comfortable. Stop singing if you feel anything uncomfortable in your throat or mouth.

- Keep the tempo, feel the beat, and sing in medium volume without getting louder or quieter during the scales or range.

Use the 2.2 scale series but sing on *bagh*, like the English word *bat*. Make an ugly sound! Do you feel vibrations in the tip of your nose? Avoid any pressure or pushing!

DEBRIEF

We are using vowel sounds to indirectly change the functions of your voice. Singing *bagh* helps you sing with more intensity but without tension. Each vowel sound has a different effect on your voice. Your ability to tactilize, audicize, and visualize will help you find out which vowels are the most effective for you.

COACHING TIP

When we're children, we're able to make many sounds with our voices without tension. As we grow up, the sound of our voice becomes aligned with our identity. This makes it difficult to make odd sounds. But as a singer, the ability to make all kinds of sounds without tension or forcing leads to expressive singing. Be willing to play with your voice and find the sounds that improve the way your voice functions, without worrying about the sound. When you master this, you can easily "polish" the sounds for the music and style you sing.

In Conversation with Mike Moore

It's time to relax. You've been digging in to discover more about your voice in this chapter. Wipe the dust off your hands, sit back, put up your feet, and take a look at this chat I had with Mike Moore, lead singer, guitarist, and songwriter for the band Fire in the Field. Check him out on Spotify, Facebook, and iTunes. You may recognize some of his experiences in your own life—and learn some fun facts along the way.

LINDA: So even though we've known each other a long time, I don't really know a lot about your thoughts on your singing and your voice. Tell me about what it was like in the beginning. What made you want to take voice lessons in the first place?

MIKE MOORE: I think I always felt comfortable playing the guitar because I had this instrument, this physical object, in front of me. Instead of just me, alone, kind of naked. In my head, I thought, *I never want to be a singer.* But in my heart, there was always an energy or a vision of being out in front and getting people excited. When I started playing guitar, I didn't realize I'd be playing other people's music. That was OK for learning, but I really want to express my own thoughts. Even in middle school I was reading poetry and writing out my thoughts—seeing the scenes play out in my head and wanting to share them with people. But even singing in choir in middle school was scary!

LINDA: That's interesting—but you weren't scared of singing alone in your living room?

MIKE MOORE: No, it was just when people were around who could hear me! I was definitely freaked out about that.

LINDA, *laughing*: Well that's true of just about everybody! Most people are scared of singing in front of people, which is interesting because, originally, humans sang for social bonding, identifying tribes, and healing.

MIKE MOORE: Yeah, it's so close to what makes us human. When I'm feeling down or whatever, if I just pick up my guitar and start singing, there's an immediate release. You're so connected to the feeling the act of singing gives you.

LINDA: There is some research going on right now that shows the vibration of the vocal cords does play a role in some kind of healing, so your feelings aren't far off.

MIKE MOORE: Yeah, like I've been running lately, and I was in this race, running and getting tired, thinking I'm really out of shape and not ready for this, and then the crowd starts cheering "Whoo-hoo!" It has an immediate effect on you, just hearing their voices. I felt like *Yeah, all right, I can keep going.*

LINDA: So how did you get from thinking you had these stories you wanted to share to taking voice lessons?

MIKE MOORE: I remember I would ask my mother and sister to come into the living room to listen to me sing something. After I sang, my mother would say, "That's great, but why don't you sing like you? Why are you trying to sound like these guys? Why don't you sing in your own voice?" She's not even a musician, but I knew she was on to something. So I had that in the back of my mind for a long time, but I didn't like the sound of my voice. I saw myself as a writer-guitarist.

LINDA: That's funny because you have a great voice. I always thought you had a great voice.

MIKE MOORE, *laughing*: Thank you. Well, that's funny. I still have my qualms—I still have my doubts.

LINDA: So, what made you want to try and check out voice lessons?

MIKE MOORE: It was actually a matter of survival! We had a lead singer in the first rendition of Fire in the Field in college, but the singer became an issue. He had an ego, and he didn't want to practice or work on his voice.

LINDA: What was the problem with his voice?

MIKE MOORE: He had just one tone. He had one high, yelling Robert Plant tone, but he couldn't use any other range or dynamics. We were probably mean to him, so he finally left. But I kept writing songs and lyrics. Then I realized we didn't have anyone to sing them. So I figured it was time to give it a shot.

LINDA: I remember when you first came to me, you were in the middle of that situation, and you came in after gigs pretty down about that.

MIKE MOORE: Yeah, sometimes he would just get drunk before gigs, so we were like "Dude . . ."

LINDA: So he had a good voice but couldn't do dynamics and other things with his voice?

MIKE MOORE: Yeah, it was a nice voice, but he wasn't willing to work on it.

LINDA: So when you started to work on your voice, what was the most frustrating thing about it?

MIKE MOORE (*long pause*): All of it (*laughing*). The whole thing, man, the whole thing. (*Laughs again.*) The entire thing. Oh, man.

LINDA: I remember you had a strong image of some great voices in your head, like James Brown, so your frustration, was it coming from you knowing that you didn't sound like those guys?

MIKE MOORE: Yeah, thank you, that's was *a lot* of it. Like James Brown and Ray Charles, oh man.

LINDA, *laughing*: Umm, it's tough when you're nineteen years old, to sound like Ray Charles.

MIKE MOORE: Yeah, those voices, they're, like, so soulful and gritty, you know.

LINDA: You know, those guys also had the advantage of growing up singing gospel music in church. It's a great tradition because they sing from real passion. They didn't grow up singing in their living room to recordings but singing in church with lyrics that really meant something to them in their daily lives. They weren't trying to make a certain sound. They were just singing to express passion. That's a lot different from listening to pop singers on the radio today and singing along with them.

MIKE MOORE: Yeah, right, no doubt about that.

LINDA. So what kept you going when you were so frustrated? I always had a feeling you felt bad about your voice, but no matter what I said, you didn't believe me. (*Laughs.*) The only problem you had, was connecting your lower range to the upper range, which just about everybody has to learn.

MIKE MOORE: I think I still have qualms about my voice, but at a different level.

LINDA: Some of my colleagues and your fans also think you have a great voice. So, it's not just me. Maybe there's part of you still comparing your voice to those great blues and gospel singers?

MIKE MOORE, *laughing*: Probably. I played a gig last week with some other singers, and a bunch of people came up to me afterward and said I had an amazing voice. I'm thinking, *Haha! That's hilarious.* And there was this girl that sang. I thought she was ridiculous—her voice was amazing. And she messaged me after the show to tell me my voice was amazing. I don't know, maybe she's just trying to get with me.

LINDA: It is interesting. I'm so curious about where that comes from. So many people feel the same way you do about their own voice. I'm just wondering, because singing is our instinct, yet we worry about it so much. We don't sit around wondering about whether or not we have a good hair color, for example.

MIKE MOORE: Yeah, I think it's because it's so internal, that's what I feel like, I don't know . . .

LINDA: And you know what's even funnier? All voices are good, and all voices sound good. It's just a matter of connecting the lower and upper ranges: Is it authentic? Is it real? If you want to have a commercial career, then there are other skills you need to develop, but it's never about whether or not the voice "sounds good."

MIKE MOORE: Yeah, I think it's about the sounds I have in my head, and what I want to come out, and the difference between that and what does come out. Sometimes that difference happens because I'm singing and playing the guitar; when I divert my attention too much to the guitar, I can go off.

LINDA: Yeah, and that can happen once in a while to everyone who plays and sings.

MIKE MOORE: So I think maybe what I'm talking about now is feeling like, How do I develop an authentic style, that is, like, "this is me" through and through. Going back to what you were asking earlier, I think what kept me going was the small victories—like, all of a sudden, a moment in a lesson when I suddenly felt something physically very different going on, inside and out. And I'm like, *Whoa, what is that? That is really cool.* Or I was at home singing to Prince or Michael Jackson, and I'm like, *Oh man, I'm not only hitting these notes, but I'm singing them, and it feels good.* Definitely, it was those glimpses of getting to the next level that kept me excited.

REFLECTIONS

o   Which aspects of Mike's experiences do you recognize in your own life?

o   Did you notice when Mike was using the processes of tactilize, audicize, and visualize?

o   Mike Moore isn't the only singer living with doubts. Singing and making music is a journey for everyone. Broadway star Idina Menzel, who played the leading role for the award-winning Broadway musical *Wicked*, said, "We don't become immune to needing to find our confidence and our self esteem, there's always something in our life where we need to remind ourselves that we are enough."[8] How do you experience this in your own life? What strategies are you using to find your confidence and self-esteem?

o   American contemporary music evolved from the music of African slaves who developed their own way of creating songs and music. They expressed their grief, pain, and suffering with their voices. They even communicated escape routes through song.[9] How does this influence the music you sing today? What does this show us about any of the differences between contemporary music and classical music?

o   As we'll discuss later in detail, our ability to make complex vocalizations and sing as we know it today evolved as part of our survival instincts. How is that evident in singing today? In your own singing?

3

CONNECT THE LOWER AND UPPER RANGES

He had a perspective on details that was unmatched. And he paid attention, and that's what you're supposed to do. That's the only way you can be great, you know, is pay attention.

—Quincy Jones, Grammy Award–winning producer, answering the question "What was Michael Jackson's greatness?"[1]

In the last chapter, you learned that every diamond and every voice has "inclusions," and that these inclusions can determine not only the beauty of your voice but also the stress areas. You learned how to evaluate your stress areas—and that you can develop your ability to tactilize, audicize, and visualize so you can eliminate them. (There may be elements of your singing that you want to keep for style depending on the kind of music you sing. You won't lose them. You'll become more authentic.)

You're going to learn an exercise to begin training your ability to move easily from lower notes to upper notes without losing tone quality or straining. Just like polishing and smoothing the surface of a diamond exposes its color and clarity, you can develop the color and clarity of your voice by smoothing the connection between the lower and upper parts of your range. To do this well, you need to pay attention to details. You can do that by focusing on your experience. What are you sensing when you sing? Airflow? Muscle? Vibration?

3.1 SCALE SERIES
Finding Connection

The following exercises train your voice to connect the upper and lower ranges so you can move easily in songs. Because singing is an aerobic activity, you may feel air pressure or compression (and a cardio workout), but it should be comfortable or effortless in every other way. If it's comfortable, continue singing; if it's uncomfortable, stop, take a break, have a cup of tea, or go for walk. Reassess what you're focusing on and review the goals of the exercise. Make note of what you're feeling and hearing. Then try again.

TRIAD WITH REPEATING OCTAVE

Sing the following exercise first on *goo*, as in the word *google* (IPA=gu)

1. Practice speaking *goo* in a light, higher, "hooty" voice, like an owl. Can you audicize the sound? Can you speak this in a higher part of your voice? Can you whistle? This is the shape of the vowel. You may feel vibrations above your mouth and behind your face, but try to keep the feeling of vibration very similar throughout the scale, without any abrupt changes.

2. Choose the scale with the most comfortable range for you. You may be able to sing higher than you expect if you keep the *hooty* voice.

3. Play the scale on your instrument or listen to the audio file.

4. Feel the rhythm! Tap your foot to the beat, relax your hands.

5. Only sing as high or low as you feel comfortable.

Can you keep the tempo? Is your stomach loose? Remember to make whistle lips!

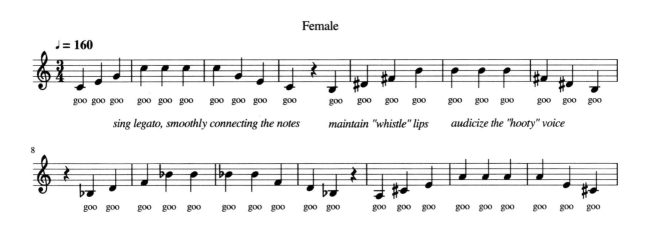

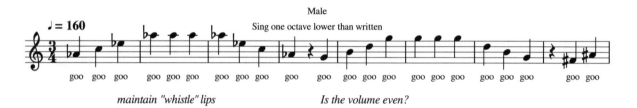

maintain "whistle" lips   *Is the volume even?*

Can you say a clear "g"

If its feels comfortable, sing back up the scale.

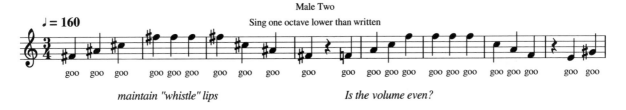

maintain "whistle" lips   *Is the volume even?*

Can you say a clear "g"

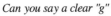

If its feels comfortable, sing back up the scale.

Chart Your Experience

Answer yes, no, or don't know.

AFTER SINGING		AFTER RECORDING
_____	Sound was very light or breathy.	_____
_____	Couldn't sing with "whistle" lips.	_____
_____	Felt pulling in my neck/throat.	_____
_____	There was a change in tone during the scale.	_____
_____	Tone felt smooth and connected.	_____
_____	Intonation was clear.	_____

Other experiences: _____

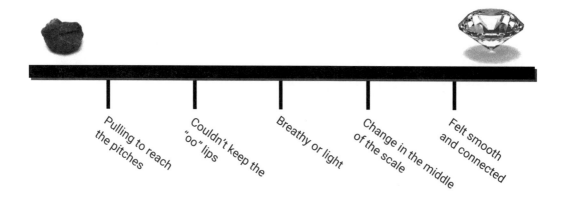

Pulling to reach the pitches | Couldn't keep the "oo" lips | Breathy or light | Change in the middle of the scale | Felt smooth and connected

DEBRIEF

Mastering clear pronunciation of the vowel, and even volume, are the keys to effortless singing. Singing with a clear vowel isn't always easy because you may have tension in your mouth, tongue, or throat. Volume can be difficult to manage if you're used to blowing a lot of air or using muscle to "reach" notes. Use your power to audicize to develop those skills.

COACHING TIP

Use a clear consonant to find consistent contact. The *g* should be firm and clear, but not pressed. The *g* will help you maintain contact in your voice. Audicize the vowel and volume before and during your singing. Tactilize how you will begin the tone. Do you need a light touch or a firm touch?

Record yourself singing the scale on audio or video. Ask your buddy to watch you or the recording. Chart your experiences again.

Now sing the same scale on *gee*, as in the word *geese* (IPA= gi)

- Practice speaking *gee* in a voice that feels "mouthy," as if you were imitating the sound of someone with a cold. This may sound a little silly, not like your everyday speaking voice; you should be exaggerating, but avoid overworking. The inside of your mouth should be passive but with a clear *g* sound.

- Choose the most comfortable scale.

- Keep the tempo, feel the beat, and maintain the feeling of singing in an exaggerated low voice, open and relaxed.

Chart Your Experience

Answer yes, no, or don't know.

AFTER SINGING		AFTER RECORDING
_____	Felt like it was pulling.	_____
_____	I sang the scale with wide smile lips.	_____
_____	Sound was very light or breathy.	_____
_____	There was a change in tone during the scale.	_____
_____	*Ee* vowel sounded clear and consistent throughout.	_____
_____	Felt relaxed.	_____
_____	Intonation was clear, I didn't hear anything get "pitchy."	_____

Other experiences: _____

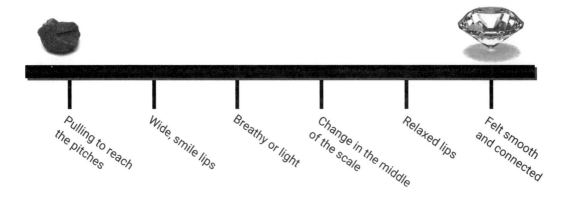

Pulling to reach the pitches

Wide, smile lips

Breathy or light

Change in the middle of the scale

Relaxed lips

Felt smooth and connected

DEBRIEF

Avoid allowing the *ee* to modify to *ih*, as in the word *in*. Do you hear the vowel changing during the scale?

Keep lips in a neutral shape—not wide in a "smile," but neutral like when you say "geese." You may have to "pout" to prevent your lips from widening.

Singing an *ee* vowel like this will limit your choices for range and tone, and it is probably uncomfortable!

Its best if you can sing *ee* with your mouth relaxed like this, throughout your range. This is possible because we make the *ee* vowel with the tongue, not the lips. Try it! Look in a mirror and say some words like *geese*—when you speak, you don't use your lips! This is important because the shape you make affects the acoustic properties of the tone. If you're having trouble singing with relaxed lips, try opening your mouth more while keeping your lips relaxed. You can use a mirror to practice.

COACHING TIP

You're working on connection from low to high in these exercises. If you are loud, out of tune, or feel tight and reaching on the upper notes, remember the hooty voice, like an owl.

Record the scale on audio or video. Ask your buddy to watch you or the recording. Chart your experiences again.

REVIEW

Listen to your recording. Did you see or hear anything different than you expected? What are the things you don't like? What are the things you do like? Did you change any of the answers on your evaluation after watching/hearing yourself sing the exercise? Did your buddy give you any useful feedback?

Now, look at the lessons with other singers working on the same scale. Do you find anything similar with your experience?

MALE SINGER

LINDA: OK, so we heard in the first scale that you have a tendency to reach up or pull up as you transition from lower to upper range. Let's explore the upper part of your voice so you can find out how that works. Can you speak *goo*, making a "hooty" sound? (*Demonstrates speaking on a high, but comfortable pitch.*)

You, *practicing speaking "hooty."*

LINDA: OK, so you are working really hard, but you don't need to. Could you speak more gently but with a feeling like the sound is coming out your mouth? This will prevent you from flipping into falsetto. Use a clear *g*. (*Demonstrates.*)

You, *in a low voice*: Goo.

LINDA: That's great! That's your normal speaking range. Could you say it higher, but not my range. (*Demonstrates.*)

You, *speaking in a higher voice*: Goooo.

LINDA: Great—that's exactly where you should sing it—use that same voice to sing. (*Plays the scale.*)

You, *singing the scale in medium volume with a clear* oo *vowel, with the sound coming out the mouth.*

LINDA: That's it. Now you just sang the same notes without reaching or trying to hit the pitch. It sounded easy, clear and I understood the vowel. That would work great in song.

YOU: Really? It felt so light!

LINDA: I can imagine that. You're used to singing with much more effort in this part of your voice. But when you do that, you are sacrificing the quality of the sound. It also costs you much more in terms of your voice. You want to find the way to sing without paying a price for it!

YOU: But what if I want to sing louder?

LINDA: Volume will evolve from the training. We're singing an *oo* vowel on the upper part of your voice right now, so it's not going to be loud. You don't hear songs with power notes on *oo*. But we do want the sound to be resonant. That's why we're using the *g* to keep your voice in contact. We want it to have the full color of your voice, and the sound to travel out away from you. We'll work on getting more vocal intensity when we do other vowels and exercises.

YOU: So, do I sing it in falsetto?

LINDA: Falsetto can help you find a feeling of release, but it won't help you develop a strong upper voice. Falsetto is very low *contact* in the voice, so, generally, the color, dynamics, and emotion you can express in falsetto is limited. There are some expressive moments when you may want to sing in falsetto for a style or particular emotion, but most of the time, you'll have more choices and feel more comfortable if you can stay in contact in your upper voice, in a light mix.

YOU: How do I know the difference?

LINDA: That can be difficult at first! If you're able to sing the scale with even volume, with any sudden changes, or "breaks," and your vowel is clear, you are most likely on the right path. When you sing in falsetto, there's a sudden "switch" at some point in the scale, and it's really difficult to hear a clear vowel.

DEBRIEF

It's difficult to sing in one voice from low notes to higher notes because your larynx can rise up in your throat with the pitches, like it does when you swallow. You can find out what this means; put your index finger on your Adam's apple, then swallow. Did you feel it move? That is your larynx rising so there's space in your throat for food and drink. But, in singing, your voice will get tired and the sound will be limited if your larynx is moving like this with the changes in pitch, and you won't be able to make a variety of dynamics or expression. If you're feeling a "switch" into falsetto or a very breathy tone, and you can't feel the resonance in your mouth, you can change it by *tactilizing* the touch of a firm handshake before you sing. No one likes a soft, weak handshake, or a tight, squeezed one. But a nice firm handshake makes everyone feel comfortable and confident. When you sing, you can tactilize that firm handshake too.

FEMALE SINGER

> LINDA: OK, so we heard in the last exercise that you sing in a very light, falsetto-type voice as you transition from lower to upper range. Let's try a scale that will help your voice stay in better contact. (*Demonstrates triad with octave repeat on* gee as in "geese"—*female.*)
>
> YOU, *singing the scale very quietly.*
>
> LINDA: OK, so I hear that you are singing the scale evenly, but the sound is very quiet and airy.
>
> YOU: Yes, I know it's quiet, but I can't get out any more sound in that part of my voice.

LINDA: OK, the easiest way to find out how to get contact there is to connect with your speaking voice. Can you say *gee* as in "geese", in a woofy speaking voice, like you have a cold?

YOU: (*Speaks* "gee, gee gee" *in a low, mouthy voice, and laughs.*)

LINDA: OK, sing with that voice. Use the consonant to help you.

YOU: (*Sings the scale. The sound is louder, but the singer is stretching with her neck and head.*)

LINDA: OK, good. You got the voice more like talking, but I can tell you were working really hard.

YOU: Yes, it was uncomfortable.

LINDA: Sometimes when you try to get more voice, you add in some extra effort that you don't really need because you're trying to make sure you get it right. If you focus on the silly voice, and a clear *ee* vowel, *before* you sing, you'll find that connection without working so hard. Sing the scale again, thinking about the feeling when you spoke *gee* in that low, silly voice. Be sure you say a clear consonant because the *g* will help you.

Developing an area of your voice that you aren't accustomed to using, or changing the way you've been using it, may be easier when you consider basic sound science.

Sound: Energy that moves through air, water, and other objects and makes their constituent molecules move in back-and-forth waves, like an accordion. These waves can be measured by length and height on a spectrograph.

Frequency: The unit of measure used for sound waves, measured in hertz (Hz).

Harmonic: A basic component of a sound. Musical sounds have harmonics at regular intervals. The first harmonic is the fundamental; the pitch that we perceive. Each musical sound has other harmonics above the sound that we perceive. These harmonics occur at the same intervals for every musical sound.

Resonance: Amplification of frequencies and harmonies that creates sound with optimal vibration.

Sympathetic vibrations: Vibrations of an object near the sound source that vibrates at the same frequency because it's nearby!

The sound of your voice has characteristics that are unique to you, but it isn't a fixed object, like a chair or a table! Sound is energy, whether it's your voice, a clarinet, or a car siren. It can be measured, and it can be modified by the source of the energy or the environment the energy moves through (water, air, wood, etc.). Your voice has two sources of energy: the airflow/pressure and the movement of your vocal folds. As the sound waves move through the "tube" of your throat and mouth, the vocal tract, they are affected by the size and shape of the muscles, tissues, and spaces within the tract.

Vocal training is mastering the ability to manage the source of the energy *and* its movement. Consonants, vowels, and high or low vocalizations change the alignment of the frequencies in the sound, making it possible for you to change the way you and others hear your singing. You can audicize the frequencies of sound, and you can tactilize the vibrations caused by sound waves.

Each sound consists of a fundamental frequency and several other frequencies above the fundamental. In Western music and singing, sound is considered pleasant, expressive, and powerful when the fundamental and its frequencies occur at even ratios. In non-Western music and singing, listeners are accustomed to more variation in the way frequencies occur. For example, the interval between five notes (a major fifth) occurs very often in Western music because the frequencies line up quite nicely, causing an increase in resonance. It's very similar to the sensation you have when you sing a clear vowel—you sense the resonance through the sympathetic vibrations in your bones, muscles, and tissues because the frequencies of the sound are *aligned*. (You can see how this affects powerful singing in the vocal tract dis-

cussion in chapter 7, page 156–157.) The interval of a half step is the opposite, the sound waves of the fundamentals are so close to each other, the frequencies above them don't line up nicely; they "crash" into each other. Even though you're singing one note at a time, rather than intervals, this is similar to the effect you can create with the frequencies in your singing.

Your hearing also affects your habits and your ability to change your singing habits. When sounds waves enter the ear, they travel through the ear canal, where tiny hairs turn them into electrical signals that are picked up by the brain; then the signals are "interpreted." Much of what you "hear" is a result of things you've heard in the past, along with whatever may be occurring in your environment and mind at the time, like surrounding noise, sympathetic vibrations, or distracted thinking. Your hearing will even "fill in" parts of the sound that may be missing—in effect, hearing something that isn't actually there, called auditory illusions.[2] This processing system is always learning, so the sounds you're hearing for the first time may sound strange or unpleasant at first, like hearing a certain genre of music for the first time, or hearing a new sound come out of your voice.

◆　◆　◆

Before you can sing powerful high notes, easily move through riffs or coloratura, dial in dynamics, or move your listeners to tears and laughter, you'll have to *practice*.

Practicing is another word for "doing." It's the word we use when we're repeating an action to improve what we're doing—and it happens in many forms, shapes, and sizes. You can practice at home, in a practice room, in a warm, misty shower, sitting in traffic, in a high-pressure rehearsal, at a recording studio, sometimes even onstage. You can practice exercises, or songs; make sighs, grunts, and animal noises; or sing through a straw. In all these places and in all these vocalizations, you are doing it—you're singing—and the experience of singing is informing your voice, body, and mind. This is practice. So you'd better pay attention.

It can be confusing to find out how and what to pay attention to because singing is a complex process. When I'm coaching new students who have been singing for a long time or had previous voice training, one of the most common things I see is misunderstanding *how* to pay attention. When I coach them to do an exercise a certain way, they do something completely different. If I asked someone to grunt like a gorilla or do a headstand, it's perfectly understandable that that person may not do what I ask—or might even run out the door! But what is going on when a coach asks a singer to sing a scale on *oo* and the singer sings the scale on *oh*? Is this just an untalented, lazy person who doesn't listen?

Of course not. It's not your fault if you haven't paid attention to the right things. The trouble is that in our fast-moving, info-laden world, your attention is get-ting *stolen*. You're captivated by the latest reality TV star, the most recent celebrity "world tour crisis," friends studying at your school, your community theater problems, opinions from your band members, the newspaper critic who saw your last gig, when your last voice teacher told you to push on your stomach . . .

What's stealing your attention? I remember my days as a conservatory student. There were so many things stealing my attention. It seemed everyone had an opinion about my voice, and the opinions were all different. My friends were singing in the opera studio, but I couldn't because I was too young. At the same time, I seemed to be getting old very fast. Was I going to be too old to audition for a young artist program? So many things were stealing my attention that it seemed almost impossible to make meaningful progress. My clients struggle with similar distractions; band members and managers criticize their singing even when they aren't singers themselves, or they're bombarded with reviews that may be good, bad, or ugly. Even today's college and conservatory students also have many things stealing their attention: a steady onslaught of auditions, ensembles and peer pressure.

Sometimes, you only learn the value of paying attention in an extreme situation. For example, scuba diving teaches you a lot about paying attention. When you've descended to the bottom of the ocean, you have to carefully look around to see where you've landed. Is your dive buddy there? What is the visibility of the water? How is the current? Are there rocks, plants, reefs? What's above you, beside, in front? There's quite a lot to take in and really look at, and memorize, because you're about to go sightseeing in a world without air. Even though you have a tank of air, your compass, and your dive plan, you had better be able to recognize where you are so you don't get lost and run out of air while you're searching for the way back to the boat.

In singing, you don't want to get lost and run out of air when you're on your way back to the chorus. Just like a compass and a dive plan aren't enough for a scuba diver, having a great voice and knowing a lot of music aren't enough for a singer. You have to pay attention to the details that help you change ineffective habits, and develop efficient new ones so you sing with a consistent, reliable, expressive voice.

Paying attention is a skill. You can train and practice how and what you give your attention to, just like you practice music. (Even if you have a condition that affects your ability to pay attention, you can learn strategies to improve it. See chapter 8, pages 166–167.)

You have choices about what you do with your attention. Don't throw it away or allow it to be stolen from you. Zero in on what you need and the attention thieves will disappear with the morning fog.

◆ ◆ ◆

Begin recapturing your ability to pay attention with vowels. Vowels are one of the most important tools you have to train your voice because they make words understandable; they affect the position of the muscles in your throat and larynx; and they change the acoustic properties of the sound (intonation and tone). You can learn to tactilize and audicize these properties.

If you've been singing for any amount of time, perhaps working with a teacher or coach or choir, you've probably gotten some (or a lot of) advice about vowels. The best way to clarify your thoughts is to go back to basics. What exactly is a vowel, and how can we use vowels to improve singing?

Each vowel comes from speech, and has its own perfect shape. The shape can be something you tactilize, audicize, and visualize. Some vowels are made predominantly with lips, like *oo* and *oh*, and others are made predominantly with the tongue, like *ee* and *ay*. How much you open your mouth also affects the vowels. So when you sing a vowel, these are your goals:

- Relaxed mouth. You should feel that the inside of your mouth is calm. Although your tongue, lips, and throat move when you speak or sing, everything should be loose and move freely. You shouldn't feel any pressing in your mouth or tightness in the back of your mouth. Both of those sensations indicate your tongue is over active. Your tongue is a muscular organ, you can learn to sing and speak without tightening it, like learning to hold a tennis racket or baseball bat.

- A clear, uncluttered sound. (Depending on the kind of music you sing, you may not always want a clear sound, but that's a style choice, not part of *training* your voice). Use your sense memory to make vowels. Maybe you will *visualize* an *oo* vowel, or maybe you will *audicize* an *ee* and maybe you will *tactilize* an *uh* vowel.

- Vowels come from speech, so "sing like you speak." Your speaking voice is the basis for everything you sing, whether you're singing rock, musical theater, or opera—connect to your speaking voice.

3.2 SCALE SERIES
What's Happening in Your Upper Voice?

This scale will further expose the coordination between the low and high voices. You have no choice but to find the way to make the connection in this exercise! Use the same tools you learned in the triad scale. If you are breathy, audicize the cackling witch; if you feel tight, tactilize and audicize the dumb, dopey dog; if you are too loud and out of tune, tactilize the hooty owl voice.

- Practice speaking *gö*, like the English word *good* (IPA= gʊ). Remember to use your lips, as if you are pouting. (*Wood, foot,* and *could* are other words with the same vowel.)

- Keep the tempo very even.

MALE chromatic

MALE chromatic

Chart Your Experience

Answer yes, no, or don't know.

AFTER SINGING   **AFTER RECORDING**

_____   I felt tight.   _____

_____   Sound was very light or breathy.   _____

_____   There was a change in tone during the scale.   _____

_____   Couldn't stay in tune.   _____

_____   Felt relaxed.   _____

_____   Intonation was clear, nothing got "pitchy."   _____

_____   Tone quality was even and clear.   _____

Other experiences: _____

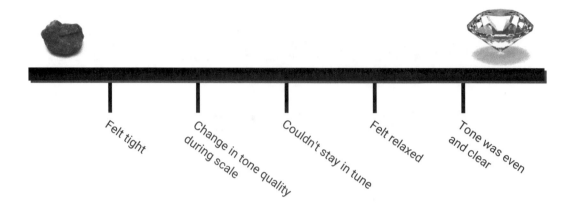

Felt tight | Change in tone quality during scale | Couldn't stay in tune | Felt relaxed | Tone was even and clear

DEBRIEF

Chromatic scales may be difficult for two reasons. First, the half step is the most difficult interval to sing! Also, the desire to move muscles in your throat or mouth may be strong. You can place a finger under your chin to find out if you're moving too much.

Male Voices: Lower male voices may find this scale more effective on the vowel *oh*, like the English word *go* (IPA = o).

COACHING TIP

If you are flipping into falsetto or a very breathy tone, go back to scales series 3.1 for a few days or a week before trying this again.

   Record an audio or video of the scale. Invite your buddy to watch you sing. Chart your experiences again.

3.3 SCALE SERIES
Descending Five-Tone Scale

This exercise helps you avoid "reaching" or "pulling" for pitches, or blowing large amounts of air. Sing the following exercise on *goo* as in the English word *google*, or *new* as in *newspaper*.

- Practice speaking *goo* in the higher part of your speaking voice. To make sure you begin singing in medium volume, not loud, imagine a sad sound, like you just missed the bus. Audicize moaning—you may have to call on your acting skills!

- Play the scale on your instrument, or listen to the audio file, even if you know the scale.

- Sing the scale most comfortable for you, tactilize and audicize moaning so you can sing with contact, but without pressing, squeezing, or reaching.

- Have fun. This may sound a little silly at first, but soon you'll feel your voice working easily, and you won't need to moan all the time!

- Tap your foot to the beat, relax your hands, maintain posture, and shake your back once or twice before you sing.

This man is a little sad. Can you audicize the sound of the moan he'd make?

GOAL

Sing smoothly, connecting the notes without big changes in volume or vowel.

Are you reaching for the first note? Try relaxing your stomach before you sing.

goo - goo - goo - goo - goo   goo - goo - goo - goo - goo   goo - goo - goo - goo - goo

goo - goo - goo - goo - goo   goo - goo - goo - goo - goo   goo - goo - goo - goo - goo

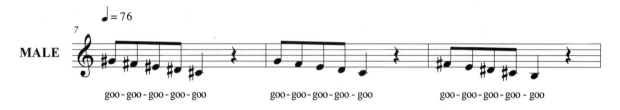

goo - goo - goo - goo - goo   goo - goo - goo - goo - goo   goo - goo - goo - goo - goo

goo - goo - goo - goo - goo   goo - goo - goo - goo - goo   goo - goo - goo - goo - goo

gee - gee - gee - gee - gee   gee - gee - gee - gee - gee   gee - gee - gee - gee - gee

gee - gee - gee - gee - gee   gee - gee - gee - gee - gee   gee - gee - gee - gee - gee

gee - gee - gee - gee - gee   gee - gee - gee - gee - gee   gee - gee - gee - gee - gee

gee - gee - gee - gee - gee   gee - gee - gee - gee - gee   gee - gee - gee - gee - gee

Chart Your Experience

Answer yes, no, or don't know.

AFTER SINGING		**AFTER RECORDING**
_____	*Oo* vowel sounded clear and consistent.	_____
_____	Tone felt smooth and connected.	_____
_____	Intonation was clear.	_____
_____	I had to "reach" or " pull" to get the first note.	_____
_____	The sound was very light or breathy.	_____
_____	I couldn't sing with "whistle" lips.	_____
_____	I had to push out a lot of air.	_____

Other experiences: _____

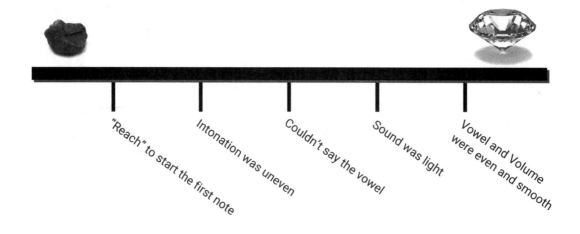

"Reach" to start the first note   Intonation was uneven   Couldn't say the vowel   Sound was light   Vowel and Volume were even and smooth

DEBRIEF

Can you practice the moaning voice with a loose, flexible feeling? Imagine you are going to sing the descending scale with the sad, moaning voice. You may have to exaggerate at first to find the feeling, but avoid forcing, pressing, or squeezing. The feeling should be comfortable, like a sad child who has dropped their ice cream cone. If you can forget for a minute that you're beginning to sing on a note that you'd rather not begin with, focus on the vowel and begin singing with a moan, you'll find the right touch to begin the tone.

COACHING TIP

Walk backward while you're singing. Make sure you have a clear path or a buddy to watch you so you don't crash into anything! What do you notice when you do this? Did anything change in your sense of singing? If you're still uncomfortable, try singing it on lip rolls.

Record an audio or video of the scale. Invite your buddy to watch you sing. Chart your experiences again.

- Now sing the 3.3 scale series on *gee*, as in the English word *geese* (IPA=gi), while you experiment with the moaning voice. You will feel the sound coming out the mouth. (Remember: we're making sounds to train your coordination, not making the finished sounds you'll sing with later.)

Chart Your Experience

Answer yes, no, or don't know.

AFTER SINGING		AFTER RECORDING
	Ee vowel became *ih*, like *in,* on upper notes.	
	I was reaching on the first note.	
	The *ee* vowel sounded clear and consistent.	
	The tone felt smooth and connected.	
	The intonation was clear.	
	Very breathy or light.	

Other experiences:

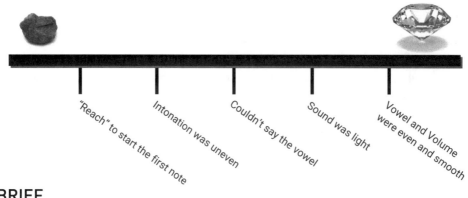

"Reach" to start the first note   Intonation was uneven   Couldn't say the vowel   Sound was light   Vowel and Volume were even and smooth

DEBRIEF

You have the opportunity to do this scale on two vowels so you can find out which vowel is easiest for you. Eventually, you will be able to sing any vowel in any part of your range, but right now focus on finding the vowels that help you sing with a clear, even tone quality without feeling like something is rising or switching in your throat.

COACHING TIP

If you having trouble finding the moan voice, try speaking with a *small amount and quiet volume* of vocal fry. The vocal fry is a creaky, bubbling sound that comes when you don't actually phonate. Many people speak with a vocal fry at the end of sentences and it's trendy in some contemporary singing styles. Generally, classical and musical theater singers avoid vocal fry because there's no resonance and it tires the voice, but speaking a *small amount at quiet volume* will help you get out of falsetto if you feel stuck. Avoid overdoing it! Just a *little* vocal fry to find contact. Practice speaking *goo* and *gee* with a *small amount* of vocal fry at the start. You can speak in a high or low range but always with medium volume and without pressure. Once you have found the contact with the vocal fry, you can stop using it. It is not a long-term tool.

Record an audio or video of the scale. Invite your buddy to watch. Chart your experience again.

LESSON OBSERVATIONS

Did you see or hear anything different than you expected? What are the things you don't like? What are the things you do like? Do you want to change any of the answers on your evaluation after watching/hearing yourself sing the exercise?

Not sure if you're doing the exercise well? Wondering if you should just blare it out, or sing softly? Look at the following coaching session with a male singer on the same exercise. Women may have a similar experience. Do you recognize yourself in this example? Can you apply any of the coaching to your own singing?

LINDA: OK, let's begin with an exercise to begin improving your ability to connect the upper and lower ranges. Make "whistle" lips like this. (*Plays the piano and sings the descending five-tone scale.*)

YOU: (*Sings* goo *but hardly any sound comes out on the first two notes; then the voice cracks and becomes louder. Continues singing the scale.*)

LINDA: (*Stops at C-sharp5.*) OK, no worries. I hear that you have very little sound coming out on these notes (*plays C-sharp5–C5–B4*), but your voice connects really strongly when you get to here (*plays A-flat4–G4*). Is that typically what happens when you sing?

YOU: Most of the time. I just don't have a strong voice there; I can get louder in a song sometimes, but it's uncomfortable.

LINDA: OK, many singers feel this way—the goal of our training is to develop consistent contact in your voice throughout your entire range. Although, there are some changes that happen when your voice moves from lower to upper range, it's an automatic process; we don't have to learn that. But we do have to learn to stay out of the way so the voice can move freely.

YOU: Will I ever be able to get more volume in that part of my voice?

LINDA: You can absolutely train your voice to go through there with the same contact and coordination as the rest of your voice. It's like learning to ride a bicycle. Try the exercise again, and this time make sure you have a clear consonant at the start (*demonstrates*), so it's like you're going to use the *g* to get better contact. OK?

YOU: (*Sings* goo *with a strong* g *and makes connection for the first note, but still cracks on the way down.*)

LINDA: Great start! Now visualize the *oo* and start with a firm *goo*. How you start the note is important: have clear intention of the vowel and consonant, like stepping onto a rock in a river. Bring the feeling of the upper notes down with you as you descend, so you don't crash.

YOU: (*Sings the entire exercise—the sound is a little softer on the upper notes, but the crack is gone and the word* goo *is clear throughout.*)

LINDA: Great job! Now you are singing right through the first transition in your voice without pulling or reaching, but staying in contact evenly. It's not perfect yet—it's a very light contact—but it's enough to go on to the next exercise.

If you can't relate to the preceding singer, can you identify what's happening when you sing? Are you beginning the scale too loud, without a clear vowel, or blowing too much air?

Review

- Singing should feel easy and smooth.
- The sound should be even, without breaks or changes in volume.
- If you're not getting enough contact, or you have to reach or pull to get sound, speak the *goo* or *gee* while "playing" with your voice; audicize moaning; try a small amount of vocal fry; or exaggerate with a dumb, dopey dog voice.
- It's OK if the sound isn't loud or professional right now. The sound will change when you continue developing the coordination.

3.4 SCALE SERIES
Triad Without Consonants

With this scale, you're getting closer to "real" singing. Can you apply what you've learned in the previous scales?

- Sing this scale on three vowels, with the first four notes on *ee* (as in the English word *geese*), the fifth note on *ay* (as in the English word *day*), then *eh* (as in the English word *ever*) as you descend.

- Keep each vowel clear and consistent.

- Feel the beat, keep the tempo, avoid slowing down or speeding up.

ee- ee- ee-ee - - - - -ay - - - eh----------eh---eh---eh---eh

ee--ee---ee--ee------ay------eh---------eh---eh---eh---eh

Chart Your Experience

Answer yes, no, or don't know.

AFTER SINGING		AFTER RECORDING
_____	*Ee* vowel became *ih*, like *in*, on upper notes.	_____
_____	*Ee* on the upper notes sounded and felt bad.	_____
_____	There was a big change from *ee* to *ay*.	_____
_____	The tone felt smooth and connected.	_____
_____	The intonation was clear.	_____
_____	The scale was easy.	_____

Other experiences: _____

DEBRIEF

This scale should feel very free and easy. If there is a big change on the third or fourth note in the scale, you're losing your connection to the lower resonance, and/or your larynx is rising with the pitches. If you're getting to the upper notes on *ee*, but feeling a lot of switching or tension on the change to the other vowels, you're making too much of a change in your lips and mouth when changing vowels.

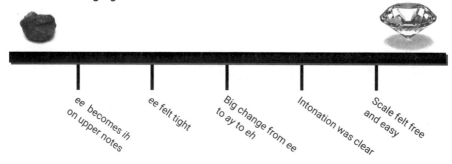

COACHING TIP

When you ascend in this scale, tactilize the sound waves going *above* your mouth. (This is imaginary, just an image to help you change your focus.) When you change vowels, keep the feeling of the *ee*, with relaxed lips and mouth open. You can also try different vowels. Begin the scale on *oo* and change on the upper notes to *oh* and *uh*.

If you're unable to keep your tone and vowel consistent, go back to scale series 3.1 until you feel sure of what's happening before trying this scale again.

Record an audio or video of the scale. Invite your buddy to watch you sing. Chart your experiences again.

Giving attention to the vowel and resonance by tactilizing and audicizing will make this exercise effortless.

4

EXTEND THE CONNECTION

Someone planted in my mind very early on, this wonderful truism called, "Fortune favors the prepared mind." Be passionate about being a musician. There is no limit to how hard you must work and how detailed you must be in every facet of what you do, either as a singer, as a musician, or as a person.

—Thomas Hampson, international opera singer

Your ability to learn a skill and perform it at the highest level emerges from your thoughts, emotions, and instincts—each mind develops its own unique connections, growing billions of synapses according to its genetics and environment.[1] You can learn a song in a few minutes, a half hour, or a day, but learning *how* to sing, and developing the ability to express what you want, the way you want, requires even more energy, focus, and attention. You've been learning that tactilizing, audicizing, visualizing makes it possible to learn more quickly and efficiently, that practice and giving attention to details rewards you with surprisingly "effortless" results, and that the anatomy and biomechanics of the voice demonstrate you don't have to push, force, or "make" your singing work. One of my students recently exclaimed in an early lesson, "Wow, it's practically euphoric when you feel your voice just come out the way you imagined it!" He is an accomplished pianist, songwriter, and arranger, but always felt uncomfortable and strained trying to get "sounds" that would express what he was trying to say. His experience of a "euphoric feeling" was his motivation to continue developing his skills—once he experienced that freedom, he wanted to have it all the time, and he wanted to be able to master his use of it.

You can learn more about this by observing birds. Birds are truly wondrous creatures. They are our closest singing relative because they share a similar neural structure for complex vocalizations. The connection between sensory perception and motor function for vocalization have not been found in other species, like some nonhuman primates (monkeys and gorillas, for example) who don't make complex vocalizations. Birds have a wide range of other amazing cognitive functions—like vocal improvisation, innovating foraging and building techniques, the ability to map out territory, and more. Not only are birds capable of complex vocalizations, most of which are beyond our own abilities, but they demonstrate high level planning, practice, attention to detail, and communication skills.[2] One fine summer day in Vienna, a friend, who was a doctoral student in bird behavior, took me to a city park to observe birds. We watched two birds of the same species competing on the ground for territory for over an hour—their planning and strategizing seemed limitless—all the while maintaining contact and communication with each other that we can only imagine. Also, I adopted a pair of canaries while I was living in Vienna. They had a cage, but I rarely closed the door, so they could fly around the living room whenever they wanted. The male canary would sing accurate copies of my singing exercises, follow-

ing up with incredible improvisation, like he was competing with me! I thought I was imagining it, but when I consulted with bird veterinarians, they confirmed that this isn't unusual at all! Meanwhile, I discovered the female secretly working on a high bookshelf, diligently removing dirt from a potted plant piece by piece in small round balls, storing and trying to hide them at the bottom of the cage. Then she collected dead leaves and other bits and pieces she'd found, meticulously arranging them in the potted plant, making a lovely nest where she'd removed the dirt, so she had a nice, safe, well-designed place where she could lay her eggs.

Many bird species have their own special skill set. (There's even a species in New Zealand that builds elaborate homes with special colors and complex architecture that appear like little stages on the forest floor.[3]) In each case where birds are observed performing a complex skill, they are observed paying attention to the tiniest details, working meticulously, and practicing until they can produce optimum results. They are highly motivated because success determines their chance to survive and thrive—the best singers and builders demonstrate intelligence, creativity, and sensitivity, so they attract the best partners. Mastery of their skills determines their chances to reproduce. They work tirelessly to achieve mastery because their survival depends on it.

The behaviors we observe in birds teach us that mastery originates as a survival skill—in nature those who are the most masterful have the best survival outcomes. We're fortunate to live in a world where we can focus on more than propagation of the species, but deep down we know what the birds know, that the benefits of mastery are wide ranging. Developing mastery in any skill empowers you—expanding self-awareness, improving overall cognitive function by fashioning new synapses, encouraging risk taking, and in singing and performing, expanding the ability to communicate universal human experiences through stories and music.[4]

In the next exercises, you'll continue toward vocal mastery by developing a stronger and more expansive connection throughout the full range of your voice. When you've mastered this scale, you will find you have also improved the overall tone of your voice, your flexibility, and your musicianship. We'll discuss all the issues that may come up when you're practicing, so you can find the answers you need to develop mastery.

4.1 SCALE SERIES
Octave-and-a-Half Arpeggio

I. OCTAVE-AND-A-HALF ARPEGGIO ON LIP ROLLS OR ANOTHER SOVT.

This scale is a powerful tool because it requires you to sing from low to high, using your whole range to develop consistency and easier high notes. If you can sing this scale without tension, you can keep your voice flexible throughout your singing life.

- Audicize the vowel *"ou"*, as in the English word *could* (IPA= ʊ)

- Even though your mouth is closed for the rolling lips, audicizing the vowel before you sing will create the muscular movements that you need to sing easily.

- Begin the scale by feeling as if you are stepping on a stone to cross a stream—so the beginning is firm and deliberate, but not loud or heavy. End the scale the same way you began.

- Do you remember the five-tone scale on lip rolls? Use the same method of placing the flat part of your fists on your jaw, just below your mouth, and push up until your lips are chubby. (This helps manage the exhale.) Take time to learn all the notes correctly.

- We're changing the volume now, practicing decrescendo (lowering the volume) as you go up the scale. Keep the lip rolls even and steady. Imagine a steady stream of air coming out your mouth.

GOALS

Move easily from low to high and return to the same pitch and tone quality as you began.

Stay musical, feel the beat, the rhythm, and the shape of the dynamics. You can tap your foot or walk to the beat while singing.

If you're having trouble singing on lip rolls, sing on another SOVT, like *vv* or *nn*.

Male One

Sing one octave lower than written

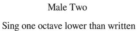

Do you feel the beat? Are you managing the volume? *Relax* your stomach muscles between scales, feel like you're "letting go" of the muscles in your stomach after you sing a scale.

Chart Your Experience

Answer yes, no, or don't know.

AFTER SINGING   **AFTER RECORDING**

_____   Lip rolls stopped at the top.   _____

_____   Lip rolls stopped on descending scale.   _____

_____   The "vowel" in the lip rolls changed to _agh_.   _____

_____   I couldn't feel the beat.   _____

_____   I sang louder as the scale went higher.   _____

_____   There were gaps in the lip rolls during the scale.   _____

_____   The lips rolls were even and felt easy.   _____

_____   The volume throughout the scale was the same.   _____

_____   Breathing felt easy and calm without gasping.   _____

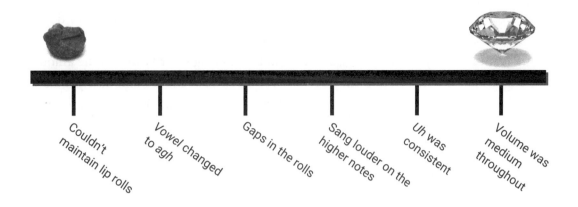

DEBRIEF

Having trouble with lip rolls? If you can't get your lips rolling or keep them rolling, there are a couple of possible reasons:

- You may need to develop a little more coordination or muscle strength around your lips. Try pressing your lips together, like pouting.

- Your vocal folds may not be able to vibrate consistently. This will change. You may want to go back to the scales in chapter 2 and practice them for a while before you try lip rolls again. Also, you can use another SOVT to practice the long scale. Try singing the notes of the scale while rolling your tongue, like a Spanish *r*, or sing the exercise through a straw!

COACHING TIP

Avoid getting faster or slower during the scale. If you're not using the recordings, sing with a metronome to be sure you're staying in time.

Record yourself singing the scale on audio or video. Chart your experience again.

One of the most basic, age-old wisdoms about singing is "sing like you speak." This classic Italian vocal pedagogy wisdom may not be as easy as it sounds. In fourteenth-century Italy, society was more contained than it is today, and they certainly didn't have TV or radio. Today, your speaking voice is influenced by the diverse languages and accents you hear, the technology you grew up with (sitting at the computer, bending your head to read a smartphone), and your family dynamics. You may speak very softly, with vocal fry, or very loudly, or without breathing very much. If you have been studying theater or singing art song and opera, you may have habits of over-pronouncing or singing vowels that are artificial and causing tensions.

Another important aspect to developing an effortless speaking voice and the ability to sing clear vowels is the amount you open your mouth and how you do it. Opening your mouth is also a motor skill— do you know how to do it? Put your index finger of each hand on the side of your face just in front of your ears. Then open your mouth, with your tongue flat, relaxed, and extended onto your bottom teeth. Open and close a few times. Do you feel that movement with your index fingers? That's your jaw joint. We use this joint to open our mouths. Now, take your fingers away and open and close your mouth with your tongue relaxed and extended onto your bottom teeth. Can you feel that joint moving loosely? If not, you can also *gently* massage the muscles from the joint down the side of your face. Use flat fingers so you don't press in hard, just lightly make circles on the surface of your skin.

Sometimes, I have to coach a singer into using their "natural" speaking voice just so they can sing more freely. Here are some ways you can do this:

- Read text lyrics or poetry out loud. Stay relaxed and read as if you were talking to a good friend in a conversational tone. You may feel moments when you feel something tighten, or take too much effort.
- Pretend you're calling out to a friend across the street, "Hey, there!" Use a relaxed voice—although you want to be heard, call out to your friend without over-preparing or using a lot of effort.
- Now, try both these things while walking around—in a room, or outside; have fun with it and try to find a relaxed speaking voice that feels like it just comes out of your mouth without extra effort and at a medium volume.

You can demonstrate your speaking voice for someone in your support network, such as a family member or friend who knows you. Read the lyrics, text, or poem from a song and ask them what they sense—even though they may not be singers or teachers, they may be able to give you some worthwhile feedback that you can apply to your own practice.

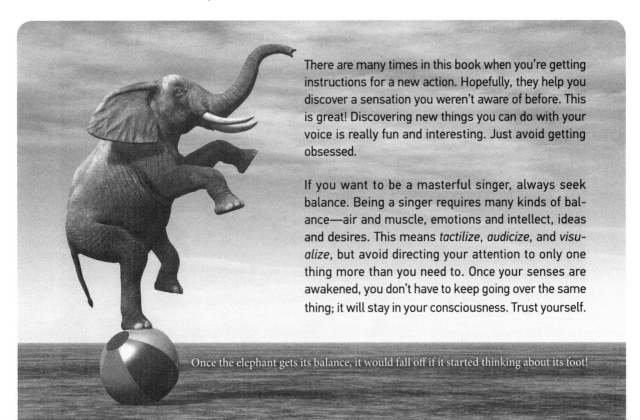

There are many times in this book when you're getting instructions for a new action. Hopefully, they help you discover a sensation you weren't aware of before. This is great! Discovering new things you can do with your voice is really fun and interesting. Just avoid getting obsessed.

If you want to be a masterful singer, always seek balance. Being a singer requires many kinds of balance—air and muscle, emotions and intellect, ideas and desires. This means *tactilize*, *audicize*, and *visualize*, but avoid directing your attention to only one thing more than you need to. Once your senses are awakened, you don't have to keep going over the same thing; it will stay in your consciousness. Trust yourself.

Once the elephant gets its balance, it would fall off if it started thinking about its foot!

◆ ◆ ◆

Being a great singer has a lot to do with flexibility of your voice, mind, and body. To develop flexibility in your voice, you need to make a wide variety of sounds. But *how* you make the sounds determines your results. There are four sounds you can use to find a resonant, consistent, powerful voice: the dopey dog, the moan, the hooty owl, and the cackling witch. Can you audicize their voices? Can you practice speaking these sounds while staying loose and flexible in the pitch of your voice? When you can say it, you will be able to sing it!

Woof! Woof!

Oh noooooo!

Hoot! Hoot!

Cackle!

II. OCTAVE-AND-A-HALF ARPEGGIO ON *GOO*, LIKE *GOOGLE* (IPA= Gʊ).

If you've practiced the long scale on lip rolls or another SOVT, you can begin using consonants and vowels that are closer to words. Remember to make *oo* like whistling. During the scale, keep your lips in *oo* and avoid changing the vowel or widening your mouth. Keeping the volume even, without getting louder or quieter, helps you maintain the *oo*.

Are you having trouble making an *oo*? Copy this man! You may open your mouth more than he does when you sing, but don't lose the *oo* lips!

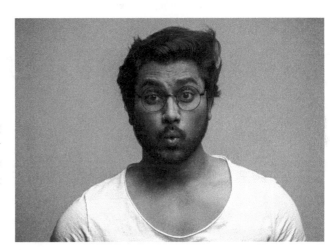

GOAL

o Use a clear vowel and manage the volume. Your singing may sound or feel "airy" or "hooty," but the pitch should be clear.

o Can you maintain "whistle" lips throughout the scale? Drop your mouth in between scales, allowing the air to "fall" in without gasping.

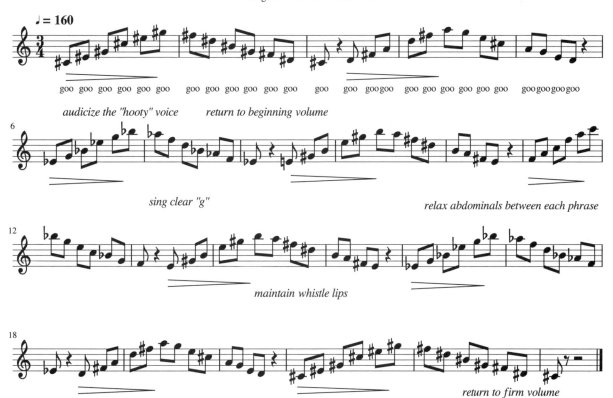

Male One

Sing one octave lower than written

Male Two

Sing one octave lower than written

Chart Your Experience

Answer yes, no, or don't know.

AFTER SINGING		AFTER RECORDING
_____	Unconsciously changed the vowel to *oh* or *uh*.	_____
_____	Louder as the scale went up.	_____
_____	Quieter at the bottom of the scale.	_____
_____	Couldn't say the *g* on every note.	_____
_____	Quieter as the scale went up.	_____
_____	Even tone throughout.	_____
_____	Strong sense of the rhythm.	_____
_____	Higher range than usual, and it was easy.	_____

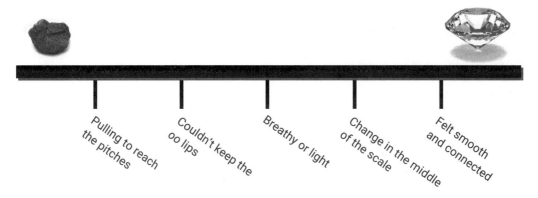

Pulling to reach the pitches   Couldn't keep the oo lips   Breathy or light   Change in the middle of the scale   Felt smooth and connected

DEBRIEF

This vowel allows you to sing effortlessly. Singing a smooth, acoustically simple vowel like *oo* is easier, allowing your vocal folds to vibrate efficiently, then you don't have to "reach" the notes or blow out a lot of air. If you're having difficulty, then *audicize* the hooty owl before you begin singing and continue to audicize while you're singing.

COACHING TIP

What about this *g* consonant? You may never have done a vocal exercise on *g* before. We're using that consonant because it helps manage the exhale and improve contact. This consonant is used in many words in songs, so you need the practice too! (Even Mozart used the consonant *g* on many high notes.)

      Record yourself singing. Chart your experience again.

III. OCTAVE-AND-A-HALF ARPEGGIO ON *GEE*

Now sing the previous scale with *gee*, like the English word *geese* (IPA= gi). Same "how-to" as in the previous scale, but this time you will experience the air moving differently. To keep the vowel consistent, you can relax your lips as if you were pouting while singing. This may be awkward at first, but as you're practicing, making movements with your lips, tongue, and jaw will become easier because it's a motor skill, just like riding a bicycle.

GOALS

- Audicize the vowel before and during singing. Eventually, it will be automatic; you won't have to intensely focus and will be as normal as brushing your teeth.

- Reduce the volume as you sing the scale but *return* to the same volume and tone at the end as you had in the beginning.

Chart Your Experience

Answer yes, no, or don't know.

AFTER SINGING   **AFTER RECORDING**

_____   Unconsciously changed the vowel to *ih*, like *in*.   _____

_____   Louder as the scale went up.   _____

_____   Couldn't say the *g* on every note.   _____

_____   Quieter at the bottom of the scale.   _____

_____   Quieter as the scale went up.   _____

_____   Tone was consistent.   _____

_____   Strong sense of the rhythm.   _____

_____   Higher range than usual, and it was easy.   _____

Pulling to reach the pitches | Wide, smile lips | Breathy or light | Change in the middle of the scale | Relaxed lips | Felt smooth and connected

DEBRIEF

Making the *ee* doesn't require wide lips. If you make wide lips, like smiling, when you're singing *ee*, your larynx may go up and you'll have less resonance, or feel "tight." Instead, try relaxing your lips, like a small pout, like talking. I'm sure you don't spread your lips into a smile when you say "geese." So if you do it when you sing, you're pulling out of your normal position for speaking—your own voice.

Can you sing *ee* with your lips like this?

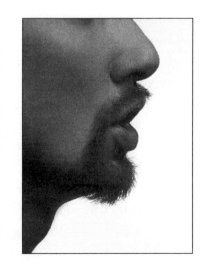

COACHING TIP

Can you "chew" while you're singing the scale? Opening and closing your mouth with the *g* as if you were loosely and easily chewing helps keep your jaw loose.

Record yourself singing. Chart your experience again.

———————

In chapter 1 we talked about singing as motor learning. We discussed how motor learning requires you to direct your attention so your brain can collect sensory information, then send instructions to muscles. This continues in a feedback loop whenever you're moving. You're learning to direct your attention for singing by using your imagination and memory to tactilize, audicize, and visualize.

Even moving the tiny muscles and ligaments of the voice muscles are a motor skill, and they can be stretched, relaxed, and trained similar to muscles in the rest of our body. That's what you're doing with the scales. It's a bit trickier than training the muscles you use when you work out at the gym, play tennis, or swim because some of these muscles are not in our conscious control. Also, the anatomy of the throat, face, neck, and chest are *highly* interconnected, and we can't see inside the larynx unless we go to a doctor. That's why you need to be vigilant when you practice—directing your focus and attention while using exercises that create changes in movements of the muscles of the throat and larynx without your deliberate manipulation. You don't need to know the names of muscles in the larynx to be a great singer, but when you are habilitating, or rehabilitating, your voice, understanding how the muscles move can help develop your ability to tactilize, audicize, and visualize.

> You can't consciously feel the muscles of your voice, but you can feel the air pressure and the muscles around them.

Basically, there are two sets of muscles that you're training—those inside the larynx that make the movements needed to vocalize and those that connect the larynx to the surrounding bones.[5] The vocal folds, two tiny ligaments, are inside the larynx. When you phonate—whether involuntarily or in speech or singing—they come together, closing, similar to hands clapping, or two flags next to each other blowing in the wind. When the air from the lungs reaches them, they vibrate, creating sound waves. The thyroarytenoid muscles (often called the TA muscles) move the arytenoid cartilage, so the vocal

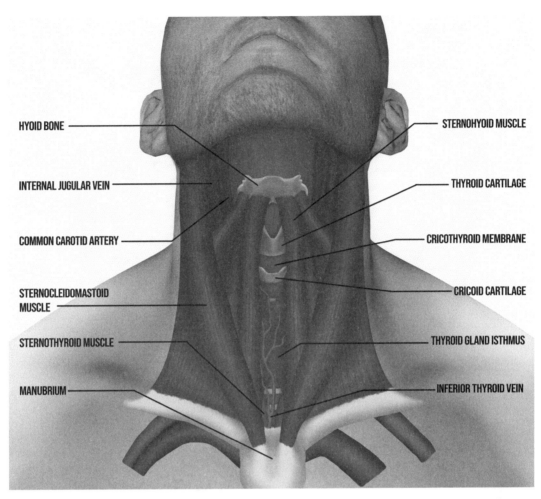

The larynx is located in the middle of your throat. This shows the muscles in your throat that raise and lower the larynx.

folds become short and thick for lower notes. The cricothyroid muscles (often called the CT muscles) change the space to make the vocal folds thinner for upper notes. The process of changing the length and width of our strings is gradual. As we sing through our range, these muscles automatically move—adjusting, moving cartilage, and modifying the length and width of the vocal folds according to the

mental plan in your mind and the aural feedback you receive while you're singing. These movements are directed from the area of our brain called the laryngeal motor cortex. It's completely separate from the area that directs all other movements (the motor cortex) and right next to the area that collects sensory information (the sensory cortex). This layout in the brain suggests that the movements for complex

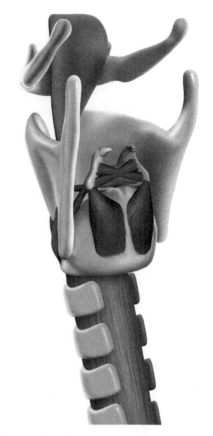

This is the front of your larynx. You can see and feel it, commonly called your Adam's apple.

The back of your larynx is open and faces the cervical spine, which also has to be free to sing easily.

vocalizations are very important, maybe one of humans' most important abilities at some point during our evolution. The part of the brain responsible for involuntary vocalizations, like yelling out in pain, is in a different part of the brain, but the two areas of the brain evolved with some connections and work together in some way.[6] Voice training allows us to have an indirect impact on these movements. All you have to do is hear the sound in your mind (audicize), imagine the sound and feeling of the vowel (tactilize, visualize), and the biomechanical system will "magically" respond. (It isn't really magic but a result of thousands of years of evolution.) The voice is an impressive mechanism. Understanding that it functions in response to your focus and training shows you don't have to reach for notes or do any complicated, mysterious movements to sing effortlessly and expressively.

In Conversation with Jennifer Maloney-Prezioso

You've been studying and practicing hard through this chapter. Now, take time to rest your mind and soak in your experiences. Find a comfortable chair, a snack or a drink, put your feet up.

In 2012 I was fortunate enough to catch Jennifer Maloney-Prezioso, the Tony Award–winning Broadway producer of *Spring Awakening*, *Legally Blonde*, *American Idiot*, and *Beaches*, when she was "between shows." We taught a workshop together in Boston at the New England Conservatory. It was wonderful to see her personal approach to coaching singers. In the workshop, Jennifer coached songs after I had trained voices. Her warm, supportive but focused approach brought out the magic. Each singer found a new way to connect with the music and lyrics because they knew they were safe, supported, and accepted. Now you can get a view from the producer's chair. What does it take to get a Broadway show from an idea to the stage? Jennifer also gives you insights about what she looks for when she auditions singers!

LINDA: So, I'm so excited to talk to you today because I think you're just such a great role model in a lot of ways—

JENNIFER: Aww, thank you

LINDA: —because of the way you built your career but also because of the many projects you do like the Groovy Projects and the way you work with people. So tell me, what are you working on right now?

JENNIFER: Right now, my main project is *Beaches*, the musical. We're going to open in the West End next year.

LINDA: Wow, yay! Congratulations. It's been a long haul!

JENNIFER: Yes, it's a very long haul, but you know it's not just trying to get it up and open. You have to make sure all the pieces are put together in the right way because when you open, you have one shot to be where you have to be for a huge success, so that the show that will go out around the rest of the world. And there's a lot of interest around the world for this title, so I just want to make sure that the production is perfect as it can be, you know?

LINDA: Nice!

JENNIFER: So yeah, so it's been a long haul, but worth it (*laughter*).

LINDA: So you've been working on building the brand of *Beaches*?

JENNIFER: Yes, and also just the team. And just doing the work. We have a new director who just came on. He needed to spend some time with the writers. The writers have been working on this for a long time, but in the past two months have written some of the most beautiful songs they've ever written for the show! All of a sudden, you have a new wind beneath the sail, new creativity comes out. It's really worth it. If you're looking for the overnight success, you need to quit theater. It's probably not the way to go! (*Laughter.*)

LINDA, *laughing*: Yeah, I think that's true about everything in the arts!

JENNIFER: Yes, I do too.

LINDA: And I'm always amazed myself how much you think something is done, and then a whole other level opens up and really changes everything; it makes it a much deeper, richer thing than it was.

JENNIFER: Absolutely, yeah, and plenty of people were like, "Oh, it's ready!" then, and I was like, "No, but there's a couple more things we can do to make it better." You also—I think that there's also a time line. Like, we know we have an opening in a year; you can't just keep working on it forever.

LINDA: True! You just said something really interesting to me—that people were telling you, "Oh, it's ready! Let's go!" and you said, "No, there's something else." What made you feel like there was something else? (Which is probably why you're the producer!)

JENNIFER: You know, there are always different journeys for how a show gets to Broadway and to the West End, but we did two developmental productions. After the first production we had tons of work to do. So when we opened in Chicago and got these lovely reviews, everyone was saying, "Oh, you fixed this. It's terrific." But all of a sudden, because we had made all those beautiful changes, I could see there were still some issues, that it could be cleaner. Then a writer had this beautiful idea. She says, "You know what? We don't need an ensemble for this show." In essence, this show is a love story about friendship, and so when the ensemble came on, it was like we were going to these other places, like we were trying to put in an ensemble. You just have to make decisions that come from the artistic place of what you're trying to create . . .

LINDA: You can just feel it when you see it . . .

JENNIFER: Yeah, and also I think it's so important for this particular story that takes place over thirty-five years. It's about friendship, and if you're not laughing, you don't deserve the tears.

LINDA: Mmm . . . Yes, true in music as well.

JENNIFER: You have to make sure the show is balanced in a way that feels all of that.

LINDA: Yes!

JENNIFER: Especially when you have a title that people are familiar with, there are a lot of people who are like, "It's my favorite movie," and they have such a connection to it—you owe it to them to get it right. We want to make sure that when this curtain opens, they feel safe. They know that these are the characters they recognize; at the same time, that they're not just getting the movie onstage. So you have to really thread that needle very carefully.

LINDA: I love your approach and attitude about that. That's really the main experience of theater and, you know, even concerts, any kind of place where we go and we sit in a venue and experience something onstage. It's about having a safe place to experience relationships and life events.

JENNIFER: Right!

LINDA: This is what performing originally was about—a chance to "rehearse" or "reenact" life experiences. And so much of what's happening today—not all of it, of course, but so much—is really about getting the quick money and getting a big name out there, so that a lot of people come and buy very expensive tickets.

JENNIFER: Yes.

LINDA: And you're not doing that, and I'm just wondering . . .

JENNIFER: Uh-huh?

LINDA: How are you managing that? You must have a team that loves you . . .

JENNIFER: (*Laughs.*) Well, it's choices you make. Because we could get big A-list stars to come in and headline this show very easily, but I also think then the whole thing becomes only about those names.

LINDA: That's right.

JENNIFER: And then people feel like, as soon as they leave, "Oh, I don't want to see that anymore," and "I feel like the star of this show is the title now." The women we had in Chicago who we're bringing to the West End are superstars, but I feel like when they play these roles, then the roles will also be stars, and people will be like, "Oh, I want to play that role." Like in *Wicked*, in the same way that it did for Idina and Kristin, the roles became the iconic part, rather than the celebrity. The easy choice is financial. If all of a sudden I say we have star A and star B, you have financing right away,

you get X theater right away, but that means the show could be over in a
year. That's just not our goal; we're here for the long haul.

LINDA: I love that it's classic old Broadway. It's the way things were done in the
past, but not so much now.

JENNIFER: Right.

LINDA: What made you go to the West End, as opposed to Broadway?

JENNIFER: You know, all my experience, most of my shows that I've done
on Broadway have gone to the West End. Some of the greats, from *Les
Misérables* and on down that have started over there and come here. When
I started looking, I was waiting for a Broadway theater. It's really a waiting game because there are thousands and thousands of shows that are
waiting to come in. And I didn't want to be in an eighteen-hundred-seat
theater; I wanted it to be more like a thousand seats because it's a more
intimate show, this story that we're telling, and also I would rather have
it be selling out every night than selling at—you know—at two-thirds
capacity. So while waiting and seeing where we were in the lineup—waiting for a theater—I just saw there was a love of this title in London that
was as great as it was here, and there was also this kind of great feeling
of *Oh, start it here!* and there was an ownership that came up that really
excited me. Then, it's about 50 percent cheaper to produce in London than
it is on Broadway!

LINDA: (*Whistles.*)

JENNIFER: It's seriously, without fail, it's between 40 to 50 percent cheaper to
do it over there. I mean, I love Broadway; I'm a Broadway girl. I will bring
it to Broadway, but I also know if we do it on West End our investors get
to recoup, and we can make sure we have a beautiful show. So now I'll just
have to go back and forth to London. (*Laughter.*)

LINDA, *sarcastically*: How terrible!

JENNIFER: Boston–New York–London commute (*laughter*), but also, in the
long term, the show is that much better.

LINDA: That's really so important and so hard to find in a lot of places today. I
love it—as a producer you are so many things.

JENNIFER: (*Laughs.*)

LINDA: I don't know if every producer does that, but you have so much that
you influence, you work with the performers, the writers, the designers, as
well the business end of it. Is that typical?

JENNIFER: No, but there are many types of producers. My goal . . . I've always been a creative producer, it's where I come from. I feel like that's where my greatest strength is. I love working with artists, like being in the writers' room or working with performers . . .

LINDA: So you must be more interested in the creative side than many producers.

JENNIFER: I feel like it's the old school producing like the Hal Princes of the world. Like with *Beaches*, I went to the writer many years ago and said I would like to do this and built the team, found the composer, worked with the writers. You know, every step of the way of putting it together, and I talk to my writer twenty times a day—and we have a relationship that is just so rare for me; if I don't think I have something creative to contribute, then it's not the right project. So yes, seeing that the vision gets out there, that's the part that I think I'm best at. I don't enjoy asking around for money, but I do spend a great deal of my day doing that!

LINDA: Yeah, it's a wonderful thing because you know people want to spend their time on the art—and producing something really creative and artistic—but you do need money!

JENNIFER: Yes, right.

LINDA: You know, you can't have great art without money, or else it's great art in a room where nobody can see it! (*Laughter.*)

JENNIFER: Right, exactly! And it doesn't do anybody any good.

LINDA: Exactly. Do you have an opening date for *Beaches*?

JENNIFER: It'll be May of next year [2020].

LINDA: OK, great, wonderful. Are you doing anything right now with the Groovy Projects?

JENNIFER: Yes, actually, I was just meeting with them yesterday. We're trying now to scale it up to the next level to make sure that it's both entertainment and an education brand. Nate's doing an album right now that's a fusion of Broadway and hip-hop music. I have a couple of television products in the works right now.

LINDA: Mm-hmm. Great, that's such a worthwhile project that can help many young people.

JENNIFER: Yes, make sure we're reaching as many kids as possible. He's done great work in Flint, Michigan, in California and New York, but now we're figuring out how to make sure that every classroom can have access to this antibullying information. It makes everyone feel two inches taller, it's a real empowerment.

LINDA: Mm-hmm. That's a fantastic project. OK, one last thing I wanted to ask you. Can you say a little about what you listen to when you hear or see singers or work with singers. What is it about them that gets you excited? When you're auditioning people for a show, what makes you say, "Oh, yes, I'm interested in this singer!"

JENNIFER: Right. I mean, what I find is, what I love about the first auditions, is the people. I think you get the best version of a performance because it's not—it's not real yet. People are taking risks—they're not as nervous. They're selling themselves in the way that they see themselves.

LINDA: OK, interesting.

JENNIFER: When you get into callbacks, and then second call, all of a sudden it's like, "Oh, this might be real. This has repercussions. This is scary." So I think the first general audition gives me an opportunity to hear what their take on themselves can be, and also have a reference in an audition room to say, "You did this thing when you first came in—I want to see more of that." If someone is great but not right for this show, I will take note, "We need to call them for this next thing," or I'll keep them in mind when somebody's asking about a particular artist. Often you're putting a puzzle together when you're casting. . . . For example, we know our leading lady for CC is 5'3". I may see somebody auditioning for the teen role who is brilliant, but if she's 5'7" she's not playing the teen version of CC. But vocally, it is about a unique tone. While I want great musicianship and knowing a singer can work with the music director, I want somebody who isn't going to sound like everything I've heard before. The two leading ladies that we're using for this show, like their voices are just . . . Their tone and their technique is so spectacular. And, they're amazing musicians, they get why their harmony needs to work at each moment, so they can do that in a very technical way but then let go of all that when they get on the stage. And the other big piece of it—it's musical theater. We do eight performances a week.

LINDA: Yes!

JENNIFER: And you have to be trained properly if you're going to last, like you can't blow out your cords!

LINDA: Singers don't always know how difficult it is!

JENNIFER: You have to learn how to sing so you that can maintain that. I'm doing a schedule right now for next week, and each of these girls has about ten songs between duets and solos. That's a *lot* of singing.

LINDA: Yes, for hours each day.

JENNIFER: Eight shows a week.

LINDA: Yes, a *lot* of singing.

JENNIFER: You know two of those days they're doing two performances. It's not for the faint of heart. If you're not trained and don't know how to use and conserve your voice—every audience needs to see the best performance and needs to see you at your best, so how do you do that? I also look to see if somebody comes into the room with a killer voice, but they've never done theater. I have to really figure out with our team, can they maintain this? Can they sing this? Are they going to belt and not be able to mix? Are they able to live through singing it over and over again? People can just injure themselves too, and just not be able to go for the long haul. Luckily, when you get to a certain level you're dealing with Broadway and West End people who are at the top of their game. They've done it, and they know how to do it. It is a skill set, so when I look and see somebody's trained and somebody's done that before, it makes a difference. Sometimes, I can hear somebody and think, *Oh my God, they're brilliant! I'd love them to sing me a song, but they're just not going to make it when it comes to the other piece of it.*

LINDA: Is that because you see that they are singing with too much effort or just because you know they don't have the experience?

JENNIFER: Well, I think some of it's experience, but some of it is if we look at them and see, "I don't know that they could do that all the time." So maybe we'll think about them as the understudy, maybe we'll see how that goes. Or if you see that they're not singing properly . . . They know that they have a great tone. They know that they have all of that, but they don't have the background of how to breathe and where their voice is coming from, and they're straining—you can hear it, you know? We have a whole team of people who are just very aware of that.

LINDA: OK, that's fabulous that you can look out for that; it is a problem.

JENNIFER: And you really have to do that. As an example, when we did *Spring Awakening*, we had all teenagers, young kids, for most of them it was their first Broadway show. And we had the most brilliant vocal arranger who made sure these kids, like every one of them, were singing so well in terms of their instrument. That's why the harmonies sounded so beautiful, because all of them were singing correctly. And then you see it on tours, or when it's not the original group anymore, you think, *Oh no, it doesn't have to be that way.* If it's done right you can really protect the voices. We were really serious about protecting those kids who were just starting their careers, you know? You don't want to destroy them!

REFLECTIONS

○ Learning what producers, casting directors, and juries are looking for surprises many singers. It's important to recognize they are just an audience: they don't want to be entertained or impressed—they want to be moved. A casting director once told me, "I get so tired of hearing people yell at me all day! It actually stresses me out!" How does this concept affect the way you will approach auditioning and performing? How can practicing tactilizing, audicizing, and visualizing help you in an audition or performance?

○ Our fast-paced culture puts a lot of value on getting things done. Have you ever worked on a role or a song and all your friends and family thought it was great, and thought it was complete, but you thought something more could be developed? How does this impact the way you may work on your craft in the future? What does the old adage, "Slow and steady wins the race!" mean when you consider your singing and performing?

5

WHAT ABOUT BREATHING?

You cannot discover new lands without letting yourself lose sight,
for a long time, of any shore.

—André Gide[1]

In the previous chapters, you've been training your voice with vocal exercises that allow you to connect your singing voice; discovering vowels can improve, or ruin, resonance; and how singing with slightly exaggerated sounds, like *woof* or *hoot*, changes inefficient vocal habits very quickly. You've also learned how to focus your attention so you can develop your sensory awareness, allowing you to learn faster than you ever thought possible. You've found your authentic speaking voice in your singing, and you've learned how to pay attention to details while eliminating distractions. You've learned that the tiny muscles of your voice have evolved to

work efficiently without your direct control, so you don't need as much effort as you may have believed. Now, it's time to delve into singing's hottest topic: breathing.

During my training as a young singer, I may have encountered every "breathing method" known to voice teachers. I was taught to pull, push, squeeze, don't pull, don't push, lift, drop, stretch, and so on. Every approach produced some kind of change in my singing. Most weren't viable in the real world of singing and performing, and some were damaging. As a teacher, I've worked with thousands of singers of many ages, backgrounds, and music styles who've had similar experiences. You may have had these experiences, too, and maybe they've caused you to develop habits like pulling, pushing, or squeezing. You may have even heard you need to "breathe from the diaphragm." In fact, the diaphragm is always involved in your breathing, whether singing or just sitting at your desk. Learning how to "breathe from the diaphragm" is a poor instruction, simply because it's impossible to breathe without it, and impossible to breathe from it. All the funny, weird, complicated instructions singers hear about breathing usually aren't effective because they disturb sensory awareness, interfering with the motor learning process and disconnecting you from expressive vocalization, which is the motive for breathing in the first place.

While I was studying in Vienna, I took lessons from a renowned American voice teacher. But after some time, I felt like I wasn't improving. Everything seemed so complicated and yet, also vague! At one lesson, the problem became crystal clear.

It was the *Tomatenmark Dose* lesson.

Tomatenmark, tomato paste, is a product many people use for cooking. (It's tomatoes that are cooked and pureed, with most of the water removed.) In Austria tomato paste is sold in very small cans because the thick paste is only used in small amounts. In German the name is *Tomatenmark Dose*—about a quarter of the size of a typical soup can.

The lesson went something like this (please don't try this at home):

TEACHER: Do you know those *Tomatenmark Dosen*?

ME: Umm. Yes.

TEACHER: Imagine you have one of the cans, but it's empty, sitting at the bottom of your spine.

ME: OK (*giggling*).

TEACHER: Now, take a breath before you sing and imagine filling that *Tomatenmark Dose* with air. When you sing, let the air spring up out of the *Dose*.

ME, *singing a scale trying to do what she said—while the lyrics from* A Chorus Line *start running in my head: "So I dug right down to the bottom of my soul . . ."*

ME, *thinking there's no way I can be thinking about this tomato paste can while I'm onstage.*

ME, *thinking something is wrong with this.*

Now, I understand that the teacher wanted me to develop a lower inhale and an energized exhale. But the tomato paste can image couldn't work, it was distracting and complicated because it wasn't relevant to the *goal* or the physical experience of inhaling. Even if you remember the image (just like I remember the tomato paste can from decades ago), you won't learn anything because it's not relevant.[2]

Fortunately, there are other ways to improve your breathing for singing. Many of you will work out your own way to breathe effectively using the exercises and concepts in this book. That's why training consistent contact is the first step towards efficient breathing. Each singer can develop their own effective way to breathe as long as the fundamental principles of anatomy and physiology aren't thwarted. The type of music you sing also determines your breathing; opera singers require considerably more air and air pressure than country singers, for example.

But many of you may have deeply ingrained habits of very shallow breathing, or the opposite, inhaling as if you've stayed underwater too long, taking huge gasps that overtax the whole system. Inhaling when you're startled, or have been underwater too long, is "emergency" breathing.

This kind of inhale happens by lifting up the rib cage so you can get a small amount of air very quickly. For singing, you need air because of the phrase, not based on an emergency, so breathing like you're surprised or startled doesn't apply. Similarly, if you sing arias and big songs before you've developed coordination in your voice, and consistent contact (see page 152), you'll have to take large gasps of air to get any results on high notes or large intervals. When you're young and have a great voice, you might sound good enough with this strategy, but you'll pay a price for it later with loss of flexibility, poor intonation, and poor tone quality.

Do you know how you breathe now? The next activities help you see how you're breathing now, so you can free you up your system, allowing you to sing great arias and popular songs without over-breathing or under-breathing.

5.1 EXERCISE
Posture Awareness

We begin with an awareness exercise. This is the way you can begin to *tactilize*—building your memory of how it feels, so you can feel comfortable and have enough air and enough air pressure when you sing.

- Stand up and place your fingers on your bottom rib, just touching the bone. Your fingers are there to observe what is about to happen. Now slouch over, like you're exhausted and hanging out on the sofa.

- What do you notice about your ribs? Is your chest and stomach sunken? Can you still feel your bottom rib?

- Notice what happens to your ribs when you slouch.

- Now stand up at attention, like you're in the army. Notice what happens to your ribs when you stand straight.

- What feels different? Is your bottom rib more prominent?

o If you don't understand, take a photo of the two positions or have your buddy do it with you so you can watch each other. Compare them. See the difference?

o Are you on course? If you're not sure if you're standing straight, think about your shoulder blades. Are your shoulder blades down? If they are down, your ribs will be in a great position for singing.

COACHING TIP

Your lungs are inside your rib cage, so if your ribs are down and leaning on your stomach, there really isn't enough room for your lungs to fill up for singing, dancing, and enjoying life. Likewise, if you're playing piano, guitar, or bass while singing, check the position of your shoulder blades. When you lower your shoulder blades, your back muscles engage. This makes you engage your chest and back muscles so you can increase your ability to inhale and exhale without doing extra work.

Now, let's improve your posture. Posture has a tremendous impact on your singing. If you have great posture, you'll have great breathing. With the right posture, you'll be able to inhale easily and fully without any complicated effort, and without any analytical thinking. Here are a few things you can do to check your posture even if you think yours is pretty good.

> **The best posture is the type that's right for your body and your style of singing. There are the rules of good posture, and there is real life. Each body is unique, and you will find the best posture by _tactilizing_.**

o Stand up. Place your fingers on your bottom rib like you did in the last exercise. Just inhale normally, there's nothing to try to do here, just inhale. You can exhale too, no need to hold your breath. When you exhale, _avoid_ allowing your rib cage to move down. Things may be moving when you breathe, but your rib cage shouldn't be moving up and down. It's OK if you feel your rib cage move when the air comes in, and its OK if you feel like nothing's happening. It just depends on your body, your condition, and your singing experience.

o Not sure what I mean? Try alternating between slouching and standing at attention again. Feel how your rib cage is moving down and up? This is the kind of movement to _avoid_ when you sing. Try singing a simple song, like "Happy Birthday," with your fingers on your bottom rib. What do you feel? Are your ribs moving up and down? What else is moving?

o With your back straight, not arched, can you notice the position of your shoulder blades? Lower your shoulder blades.

o Not sure what I mean? Make a hunchback. Now stand straight. You just lowered your shoulder blades! How does that feel? You may feel like you're standing taller than usual. It should feel easy and comfortable, even though it may be different from the way you usually stand.

Improving your posture not only has dramatic impact on your singing, but can also change your life! In my second year of voice teaching at a conservatory, I was assigned a nineteen-year-old tenor who had sung in a boys choir for many years. His voice had become stuck from years of soprano singing so we began by working on connecting the lower and upper parts of his range. It was difficult for him to make changes because he had a severe hunchback posture. I waited a few weeks before asking him about it because I didn't want to make him even more self-conscious than he already appeared to be. When I finally asked him about his posture, he told me that he'd had the problem from childhood. His mother had taken him to several doctors and physical therapists but nothing had improved, and his mother was told the hunchback couldn't be corrected. This young man had a gorgeous voice and an interest in opera and musical theater. He was a talented actor with a lovely voice. I asked him if he was willing to try a few exercises to work on posture. He shrugged his shoulders, saying, "Sure, but it won't work." He was completely shocked to see that the hunchback noticeably improved within a few minutes! He was so excited, he practiced the exercise every day. When he came to the next lesson, he looked great, and other students at the conservatory began commenting on him—" What happened? He's so good-looking now!" He was already performing regularly in musical theater but still having trouble maintaining his posture, so we made an agreement that I'd attend his performances and sit in a place where he could see me while he was singing. Then, I'd give a tiny hand signal when his posture failed. Within a few months, his

"hunchback" (a true hunchback is collapsed vertebrae; this singer's spine was bent but the muscular training straightened it) was completely gone and he was more confident in every aspect of his life. Later, he told me when his mother saw him, she cried. He's now almost forty years old and still performs regularly in opera and concerts throughout Austria and Germany.

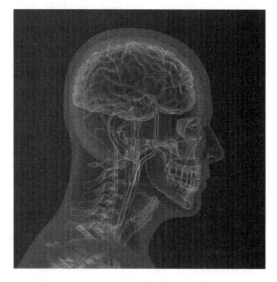

The spine of your neck needs to be in a natural position so your larynx can move freely when you sing. If your head is too far forward, or your neck is arched, it will be difficult to maintain good posture, and your larynx won't be free to move when you're singing. Put your hand on the back of your neck. Is it flat, or do you feel an arch? The back of your neck should be flat, not bending down as if you were looking at a cell phone or arching back as if you were looking at the sky.

All these exercises help you become aware of the muscles you use to breathe. What are your habits? Take a video of yourself singing and answer the following questions.

Chart Your Experience

Answer yes, no, or don't know.

_____   Ribs go up when I inhale.

_____   Stomach is tight.

_____   Stomach pushes out when I inhale.

_____   Chest collapses when I sing.

_____   Stomach squeezes in when I sing.

_____   Chest expands when I inhale.

_____   Core muscles engage when I exhale.

_____   Inhale feels easy, and "down."

_____   Ribs stay in the same position when I exhale.

_____   I feel a connection to my lower abdomen when I exhale.

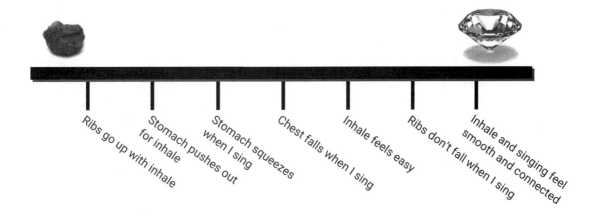

COACHING TIP

Repeat this exercise a few times until you feel like you can inhale without lifting up your ribs or pushing out your stomach, and you can exhale without dropping your ribs or squeezing your stomach. Other parts of your torso may move. Can you feel the muscles around your lungs moving? If you don't feel anything yet, that's all right. The movements will develop over time as long as you maintain posture.

There are two areas you need to develop for breathing while singing: capacity and ability. Capacity, the volume of air, is developed by improving the inhale. Ability, managing the exhale (while you're singing), is developed by improving coordination and strength. It can be confusing to find out which aspect of your breathing needs to be developed—sometimes you need both. Just like training your voice, training your breathing requires you to consider *how* to do it, rather than *what* to do.

Both capacity and ability improve from vocal training and singing. Have you ever learned a new song and found it very difficult to sing without struggling for air, and then, over time, it has become easier to breathe? That happens because the brain is very good at learning how long you have to sing without breathing, just like when we speak. We hardly ever run out of air when we're speaking because the brain has calculated how much air you need for your typical speech patterns. With every sentence, sneeze, cough, or yell, our brain calculates how much air, or air pressure, we'll need. The same thing happens when you sing—

when the song is new, it takes a short time for the brain to learn the phrasing before the amount of air can be calculated. That's why having enough air is rarely a problem. But, if there's tension in your vocal tract, or your voice isn't maintaining consistent contact while singing, the air will escape very quickly, so you run out; you had enough air for singing, but it escaped too quickly. When you sing with consistent contact, like you're learning from the vocal exercises, your ability to manage exhaling improves. As you learn more songs and get more experience, your capacity and ability will increase, and you'll be able to move your breathing muscles easier and more energetically.

◆ ◆ ◆

Breathing is a lot like wind.

Wind is a result of a change in atmospheric pressure. When air pressure is low in one area, the air is pulled from a high-pressure area. On a windy day, we see tree branches bending as if wind is blowing across, but in fact, the wind is being pulled or "suctioned."

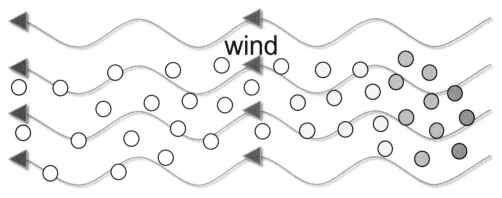

Low-pressure system

High-pressure system

Bodies work in a similar way. When the lungs are empty (there is always some residual air in the lungs or they would collapse), the air pressure on the outside is greater than the air pressure inside, motivating the muscles around the lungs to contract. These muscles increase the volume of the lungs so air is "suctioned" into them. The lungs themselves are passive—the muscles around them are responsible for expanding or shrinking them. Contracting the muscles around the lungs (see images following), causes inhalation, and relaxing them causes exhalation, thus reducing the air pressure so the diaphragm is motivated to start the inhalation process.[3] (There are other motivations for breathing, such as when our cells are low on oxygen, there is a neurological signal that motivates the inhale, but the body movements are the same.)

In other words, breathing is a lot like wind.

You don't need magical body movements to learn "how to breathe." You do need to become skillful at contracting and relaxing the muscles of your torso while maintaining good posture. You can begin by noticing a sensation of "dropping" or "releasing" when you inhale. With practice, you can drop very quickly and easily. This is a very small movement, especially when you are just beginning to notice it. You may not even feel the inhale at first, just like you don't feel it during your daily life. Within a short time, you will get stronger and more coordinated with the dropping for the inhale. If your music includes a lot of intervals, high notes, or sustained phrases, then you'll need to develop a greater capacity and ability, but that will happen gradually as you train your vocal abilities and experience more songs.

The muscles that drop, release, or generally move, allowing you achieve freedom with your breathing, include every muscle in your torso; the diaphragm and inter-costals, and the latissimus dorsi, trapezius, transverse abdominis, psoas, pelvic floor, and abdominals.

Your diaphragm is shaped like a para-chute. Notice, despite what you may have been told before, the diaphragm isn't located behind your stomach. It's located inside your ribs, attached at one point to the front of sternum (your chest bone), where someone may punch you in the stomach. It's also attached on the back. The rest of the diaphragm is unattached and can freely move. It moves down, causing inhalation, and moves up, causing exha-lation. This image shows the diaphragm at rest. If you're squeezing your stomach when you inhale or sing, the point where the diaphragm attaches to the ribs is con-stricted and the diaphragm won't be able to move down freely. If you're lifting *up* your rib cage when you inhale, the diaphragm also won't be able to move *down*.

The intercostals are muscles between your ribs. There are two sets: one for inhaling and another for exhaling. These muscles get stronger and more coordi-nated with experience. Posture determines whether or not these muscles can contract effectively to inhale. Strength determines how long they can stay contracted during singing (the exhale).

The transverse abdominis, the black muscle in this image, extends almost the entire length of your body. It originates at approximately the same area where the

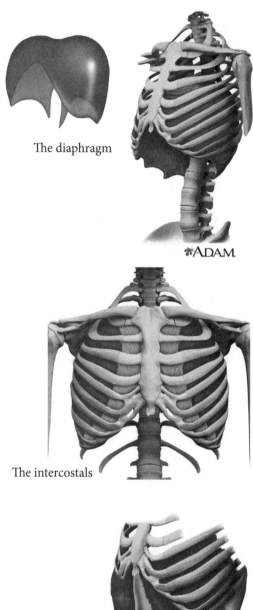

The diaphragm

✤ADAM.

The intercostals

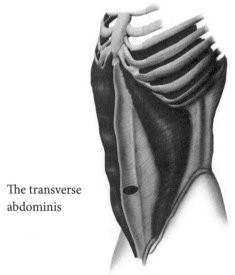

The transverse abdominis

diaphragm attaches to the ribs and inserts approximately at the pubic bone. You engage this muscle when you stand, when you do heavy lifting, and when you exhale for singing.

The back muscles attach at the pelvic floor and the arms. You engage the back muscles when you breathe, too. All the muscles in our torso are connected, and they all play a role when you breathe. Your psoas also plays a role in your breathing. This muscle also has a point of origin at your sternum, near your diaphragm. If your psoas muscles (often called hip flexors), are tight, your ability to inhale and exhale will be limited.

◆　◆　◆

As long as you are healthy, without any illness or physical condition that affects your lungs, rib cage, or any of the muscles of your torso, you don't need to learn complicated, awkward things to do with your breathing. But if you need to change old habits, or you want to develop your capacity and ability more quickly, the following exercises strengthen, stretch, and relax all the muscles of your torso so you will be in great shape for singing. They were developed by a physical therapist for patients with poor respiration due to illness but have been highly effective with singers and speakers, especially those with chronic tension in the intercostals and abdominals, or a weak pelvic floor or transverse abdominis.

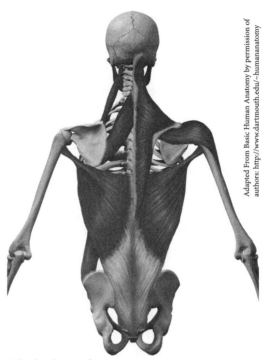

The back muscles

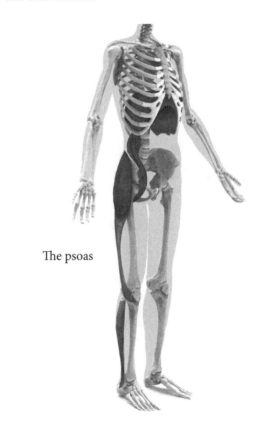

The psoas

5.2 EXERCISE
Posture and Respiration

These exercises develop your capacity and ability by inhaling and exhaling in different body postures.[4]

Get on all fours on the floor or on a bed. Your back should be level. If you're alone, you can place a small book or other flat item between your shoulder blades to be sure your back is level. Your head should also be level. Hands and feet should be flat on the floor.

Without moving your legs or arms or wiggling your torso at all, inhale through your nose. The inhale should be energetic. Fill your lungs with air.

When you've reached the end of your inhale, exhale through your mouth while continuously pulling in your lower abdomen, below your belly button. The exhale should be fast and energetic. Your torso should be stable.

When the exhale is finished, *wait* three or four seconds for your diaphragm to fully return to resting position before taking the next inhale. Pull in your stomach *below* your belly button while you quickly exhale through your mouth. One smooth movement.

You can repeat this five to ten times, pausing after each exhale to allow the diaphragm to fully relax.

VARIATIONS: RAISING ARMS IN DIFFERENT DIRECTIONS

1. Inhale as above. At the same time as you pull in the lower belly and exhale though the mouth, lift one hand off the floor. Do not allow the torso to sink to one side or wiggle.

   Return the hand to the floor and lift the other hand. You can lift each hand during one exhale, or lift each hand a few times as long as your exhale lasts.

   Repeat five to ten times, allowing the diaphragm to fully relax after each exhale.

2. Inhale as above. At the same time as you pull in the lower belly and exhale though the mouth, lift one hand off the floor and reach behind, so your arm is aligned with your torso.

   Repeat with the other arm and alternate arms as long as the exhale lasts. Do not allow the torso to sink to one side or wiggle.

   Repeat five to ten times, allowing the diaphragm to fully relax after each exhale.

3. Inhale as above. At the same time as you pull in the lower belly and exhale though the mouth, lift one hand off the floor and reach your arm to the side so that it's perpendicular to your torso.

   Repeat with the other arm and alternate arms as long as the exhale lasts. Do not allow the torso to sink to one side or wiggle.

   Repeat five to ten times, allowing the diaphragm to fully relax after each exhale.

4. Inhale as above. At the same time as you pull in the lower belly and exhale though the mouth, lift one hand off the floor and reach your arm in front of you (like a hunting dog pose).

   Repeat with the other arm and alternate arms as long as the exhale lasts. Do not allow the torso to sink to one side or wiggle.

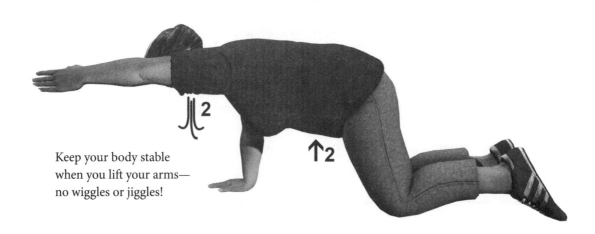

Keep your body stable when you lift your arms—no wiggles or jiggles!

Repeat five to ten times, allowing the diaphragm to fully relax after each exhale.

5. If you are already very fit, or after you've been doing these exercises for one or two weeks, you can begin using very light weights during the arm movements. Start with one to two pounds and slowly increase the weight over time.

———————

But breathing easily and effectively is much more than muscles and coordination. Breathing is tied to our emotions. And, it's likely that the way we breathe is also influenced by our survival instincts.

When new students come to me for lessons, the first topic they want to talk about is breathing.

Yet singing comes from your voice, not from the diaphragm. You'd think that the voice, or vocal folds, or larynx, would be the primary subjects singers and voice teachers would want to talk about! Strange, isn't it?

My experience shows that we often talk about it, sometimes obsessively, because breathing and posture are deeply rooted in our *instinctive* behaviors.

Almost everything that takes place in our mind shows in our breathing—when we're tired or depressed, we slouch and our breathing is shallow; when we're afraid or panicked, we hold our torso tense and breathe quickly; when we're startled or surprised, we gasp; when we're thinking analytically, we hold our breath. We know that thoughts and feelings show in your speaking voice, but they also show in your

---

"How do I get more air?"

"How do I breathe from my diaphragm?"

"How do I breathe to sing better?"

"My problem is that I breathe from my chest instead of my stomach."

"There's something wrong with my body. I get exhausted right away and can't get any air."

breathing and singing. Understanding *why* that happens may help you become a masterful singer.

◆ ◆ ◆

The intense experience of singing is not only an intricate mosaic of anatomy, physiology, and cognition but also part of our survival instincts. Although we can survive without it now, singing played a major role in allowing early humans to thrive. Today, we want to sing to share our emotional experiences and messages with others, but for early humanoids and humans, vocalizing was very serious business. When our prehistoric ancestors came down from the trees (predecessors of humans lived in the trees with birds) they were at a disadvantage because they were small, lacking large muscles and big claws and teeth like most other mammals. They needed a powerful tool and strategies to compete. Hunting, warding off predators, defending territory, mating, healing, nurturing, and identifying friends, family, and enemies motivated vocalization, especially in groups—the original source for loud vocalization or belting! What better way to fend off saber-toothed cats on the African savanna than with large groups of humanoids yelling and screaming—with weak bodies, small teeth, and no weapons, vocalization was their only defense.[5] Even today, there are examples of this strategy. At this writing, there is a terrible refugee crisis in Myanmar, near Bangladesh, India. There are many camps for the Rohingya refugees, but they happen to be located directly on the migratory route wild elephants have been traversing for millennia. Unfortunately, a twelve-thousand pound elephant walking through a refugee camp in the middle of the night is frightening, causing panic in both people and elephants. Several people were trampled to death. The UN refugee group, UNHCR, quickly established elephant response teams. When they see an elephant approaching the camp, a trained group bands together in a circle with an opening in the direction they want the elephant to move, and they lead the elephant's exit by yelling and screaming loudly! They have improved the system by using flags and sirens, but their first instinct was to use their voices.[6]

Singing is not just an emotional experience. Locating food, defending against predators, and continuing procreation are high-stakes activities; they're required for survival. If we consider that vocalization evolved as a tool for these activities, then we may have quite a different perspective on our own singing. Life or death reactions, behaviors that result from threats or in defense, take place in a cognitive state that is unconscious, where instinctive behavior takes place, rather than in the conscious mind where fear and anxiety are experienced. If you're afraid, you can talk to a friend or family member or take some action that will reduce your fear. But if someone is standing on the ledge of a skyscraper ready to jump off, they usually can't be "talked down off the ledge" because their cognitive state is inaccessible—they can't be reached by talking. People in this state often can't even hear what someone else is saying because the amygdala is controlling their sensory perception. We currently don't have direct access to the amygdala. The person can't be talked down because their state of the mind can't be brought into consciousness, like an emotion you may have when you are nervous or scared from events in daily life.[7]

The extraordinary evolution of our intricate systems for hearing and vocalization further demonstrate that these abilities must have been *vital* to our existence. Our ability to transmit a limitless array of subtle but distinct emotions, timbre, and tone in speech and singing, while the listener perceives them in an equally limitless array of interpretations, is a powerful survival tool. Even though our prehistoric ancestors didn't have physical qualities that would give them an evolutionary advantage, their *voices* gave them an advantage. And, we see the evidence that breathing and singing are rooted in unconscious responses to threat and defense even today—whether you're in a practice room, at a lesson, a rehearsal, or a performance.

We know that all mammals vocalize for basic communication—like expressing pain, fear, danger, and excitement—perhaps even for health. These are involuntary vocalizations that originate in the brain stem of all mammals. But why have humans evolved with a complex larynx that can perform complex movements for melody and rhythm? Unfortunately, we can't go back in time and ask early humans why and how they sang or vocalized, but we have circumstantial evidence, and we can observe the behaviors of birds, our closest singing relative. (Nonhuman primates, like apes, don't have the capability for complex vocalizations!) Birds use singing to experience their world. They recognize location and environmental conditions, find a mate, and keep their children together. Birds identify their family, friends, and enemies by song, so when they are flying, they can stay safe. Throughout recorded time, humans have similarly used singing to share emotional experiences, calm fears, keep the tribe together, and find mates. In ancient times, people chanted for social bonding and healing. Later, entirely separate and distinct cultures around the globe have sung "serenades" to court their lovers. For thousands of years, families and tribes have been singing together to celebrate events and rituals, like weddings and funerals. The world's ancient religions use song for prayer, meditation, and healing.

Also, current research and fMRI's show that emotional experiences shared in singing enhance cognitive function and release "feel-good" hormones.[8] That certainly would have played a significant role in how well humans survived and thrived in hostile environments.

Today's contemporary music, despite the emphasis on entertainment, has evolved from spirituals, songs created by enslaved Africans to express their suffering, to identify each other during escapes on the Underground Railroad, and provide solace; a powerful demonstration of singing as a survival tool.

Opera, Broadway, and contemporary songs focus on stories of love: unrequited, tragic, blissful, vengeful. Congregations bond through songs; nations sing anthems; and enormous audiences of many thousands spontaneously burst into song at sporting events and rock concerts—everyone knows the lyrics and melody. You can see these behaviors influencing our lives; huge concerts, obsessive devotion to celebrities, internet sensations, and our ubiquitous music scene, singing is a *still* a driving force for social bonding, sharing emotional experiences, bonding families, and creating personal relationships.

This perspective has far-reaching implications for our behavior as singers and voice teachers, whether we're learning, rehearsing, auditioning, or performing. If you feel like your singing isn't going well, then your *instincts* for social acceptance may be triggered. The need to be part of a "tribe" and be accepted isn't just psychological; it's a basic survival instinct. For early humanoids, survival in isolation or without a "tribe" would have been impossible, so sharing emotional experiences and being accepted by the tribe was vital. Even

in modern environments and cultures, humans cannot thrive without a sense of belonging.

So while singing evolved as a tool for early humans to survive and thrive in hostile environments, survival instinct is still driving our singing today, whether your tribe is your family and friends, or ten thousand fans.

◆ ◆ ◆

When you consider that singing is driven by unconscious needs, you may wonder how you can ever manage to make changes to your singing—we can't "reach" into the amygdala and sort things out the way we'd like. Fortunately, humans are not stuck responding to our survival instincts on a daily basis. We can use the perceptual learning powers of our highly evolved mind to develop new neural networks so we have more choices for singing, and every aspect of daily life.

By focusing on tactilizing, audicizing, and visualizing, you can unlock your instinctive responses. Then it becomes easier to practice connecting to your singing without fear or judgment, to practice breathing with freedom and strength, to practice *acceptance*. Accept *who* you are, and *where* you are, on this odyssey. Accept that mastering your craft will lead you toward singing with the sound and expression you deserve. Accept that training and practice will develop your craft the same way it has for thousands of other singers.

All you need to move beyond your survival instincts and toward acceptance is a sturdy toolbox and courage to lose sight of the shoreline. If you want to broaden your experience, to develop your abilities and capabilities, to become all that you can be, you have to agree to let go of the experiences that are familiar. We hear this advice over and over again in song texts and lyrics in widely diverse music spanning thousands of years. Consider texts from ancient religions, to opera, gospel, musical theater, country, rock, pop, R&B—you can find songs encouraging the listener to move on, have courage and hope, to accept change.

The exercises and concepts in this book provide the toolbox you can carry with you throughout your singing life. But you must find courage in your own heart. Having courage doesn't mean you're perfect; it means you can move forward even when you aren't, even when you can only see a few steps in front of you, even when you have to feel around in the dark to find the doorway.

Breathing isn't only about working on posture exercises and strengthening your coordination; it's about having courage to head out on the open seas, even when you lose sight of the shoreline, because you know you can discover new lands, bask in the sunlight, or dive to great depths, sharing your message with the world.

In Conversation with Dr. Ingo Titze

When I was a student at New England Conservatory, knowledge of vocal anatomy, function, and singing cognition was minimal compared to today. Much of the knowledge we have now comes from the work of a scientist who is indeed the world's leading researcher on the voice, Ingo Titze. Dr. Ingo Titze is considered the "rock star" of the vocal science world. His natural curiosity compelled him to apply his training and education to understanding the voice and spreading that knowledge in the voice community. He pioneered education in voice science in the United States. Among other things, he founded the National Center for Voice and Speech and the Pan American Vocology Association. Having studied Titze's books, listened to him speak at conferences, and talked with him about voice on several occasions, I became very curious about what motivated him to dedicate his life to searching for the "why" behind singing. What makes a vocal scientist tick? I invited him to an interview for this book about the "non-science" reasons for singing and we arranged the following Skype interview. Dr. Titze has taken voice lessons with Seth Riggs and his protégés.

LINDA: I am wondering how growing up in Germany during World War II affected your perspective, and how that may have affected your concept and hearing of voices and sounds. That was a very traumatic time for the world, the most traumatic event of the twentieth century, and I'm wondering how you think that affected your understanding and feeling of the voice, especially when contrasted with the music you heard at home.

DR. TITZE: Well, I have always walked two parallel paths in my life. Early on, I learned a lot of music, mainly folk song, classical lieder and opera. I was introduced to them by my mother, my aunt, and my older brother—they were forever telling me what radio station to listen to and feeding me pieces of music. So I got hooked. I always wanted to sing opera, Fritz Wunderlich was my favorite singer in the '60s, and Jussi Björling was another favorite. At the same time, my father wanted to emigrate to the US and wanted us to have lots of opportunity for jobs, so he encouraged me to go into the sciences. So I did six years of electrical engineering—then got hooked on physics. So I did my doctorate degree in physics. Consequently, all my life I've been figuring out which field should provide my income—the singing or the science. It turned out it was a little easier to make a living as a scientist while doing the singing as an avocation. But at some point I could not keep the two separate. I worked for the Boeing Company, North American Aviation, and Argonne National Laboratory for several years. I often sat at work and did what I had to do, but my mind always turned to the voice. I could never get the science and the physics of voice out of my mind. So I continued to explore and finally said to myself, "I've got to get some more education." I decided to study acoustics. So I went to a school where Harvey Fletcher had just semiretired, BYU. Fletcher was the founder of the acoustics research labs at Bell Telephone Labs. I needed to learn a bit from both him and my eventual mentor, Bill Strong, who studied acoustics at MIT. So there I'm in my early thirties, now finally merging the science and the art of singing. It's been a wonderful journey ever since.

LINDA: That's so interesting because those of us who know you as the "rock star" of the vocal science world could never imagine you working behind a desk at Boeing. (*Laughter.*) When you were younger, you also had this event when you were horribly struck by a hand grenade. Do you remember it?

DR. TITZE: Oh, yes. Well, one never knows exactly if one remembers at four years old directly, or remembers people talking about it, but I do remember stepping outside with my oldest brother, and he was instructed to never take me more than a few steps, because there was ammunition everywhere. We were in East Germany, and there were major war scenes going on and airplanes flying over, so we were always instructed to stay right in front of the house. But once we did go a little bit further, and there was a young boy who apparently had found a small grenade, and he played with it and capped it and ended up throwing it right in front of me. I happened to actually be bent over at the time, and I got the full brunt of the explosion.

My brother was standing next to me. He got shrapnel on his legs and so forth, but I lost my left eye, and I was wounded from head to toe. All of those healed, but the eye never did. We didn't even have an ophthalmologist or anybody that could work on the eye because all the people that had medical training were in the war.

LINDA: I can't even imagine how you got medical treatment for any of your wounds. It must have taken months to recover.

DR. TITZE: Yeah, actually, my mother just wrapped me up in blankets, put me in a buggy and rolled me to the hospital. They patched me up as best as they could; all the doctors were on the frontlines or war zones at the time, so we had limited medical help. But then the other situation was when I was born—my father wasn't there; he was in the war. My mother was very proud of me and she stuck me out the window to show the neighbors with basically nothing on and a big wind gust came up, and she claims that ever since then I had an issue with my voice, and I wanted to show her that that wasn't so. (*Laughter.*) This is why I kept working on my voice (*laughing*)— to not make that come true.

LINDA: Yeah, from what we know today, it's hard to believe that any infection you got then could permanently affect your voice but as a mother . . .

DR. TITZE: Yes, she didn't know any different then.

LINDA: So that very traumatic event. I'm curious if you think that had any impact on your love or interest in singing. What was going on in your family around that time of your injury?

DR. TITZE: Well, we sang a lot of German folk songs. Today's Germans think they're kind of cheesy actually, but in those days we sang many wonderful folk songs. That led me to Schubert and Schumann lieder, and I tried many of them—and I also got an accordion one Christmas, so I started to accompany myself. We didn't have a piano—there was no room and no money for them. But that far we did go—we played recorders and small instruments.

LINDA: But when you were injured, do you remember singing around the time when you were injured, when you were four?

DR. TITZE: Oh yes. I mean, that was the only way we could calm ourselves down and give ourselves encouragement for what came, it was so uncertain what would happen to any of us—ultimately we were refugees to West Germany, and we were just packed into cattle cars, and shipped off. It took years to find all the relatives—some in Hanover, Munich, Frankfurt—we were in Westfalen, in the Rurhgebiet. It took a long time to find each other. We were lucky to stay together as a family, because sometimes they would just shove people in the train; if somebody didn't make it, they were just put on the next train, and you never knew where that next train went.

So I think singing was a level of comfort and joy that—umm—there was just no other way to do it.

LINDA: The reason I'm asking is because it seems that singing has a big impact on PTSD in various situations. There's very little research, but it's an area I'm interested in—I can imagine that as you said in your family, with so much stress and recovering from your injuries, that it was a kind of self-medicating—we know what an enormous effect singing has on neural activity.

DR. TITZE: Yeah, and the vibrations that are created in the head by singing stimulate a lot of tissues and allow better fluid transfer. It is literally an exercise. You know, I always ask the question, If you were alone on a desert island and you had no other humans there with you, would you still vocalize? I ask that when I go lecture, and about half the people raise their hands. And then I ask, "Why?" Usually, the answer is that it just feels good; it makes my body invigorated; and makes head feel better and everything overall. So I think there is more to singing than just vocalizing for communication—it's for general health.

LINDA: Yeah, I feel the same way, I've tried to find studies about this, but I haven't found much.

DR. TITZE: There are beginning to be studies. We just finished one to do with hormone upregulation in the thyroid. We took cells from the thyroid; we stimulated them in vitro with vibration and looked at what they produced. And, certainly, they did produce hormones in greater amounts than they did without the vibration. So that's one study, but other people have studied and shown that singing steadies the heartbeat, and Jindrak wrote a book that claims the vibration stimulates the fluid movement between the blood-brain barrier. The vibration of the skull seems to help that which removes waste products from the brain.

LINDA: I'm really interested in why we sing. This is what attracted me to your experience growing up in the war because what your family was doing—it was part of your survival instincts to not only feel good but to be together as a family; you had this music that bonded you all together.

DR. TITZE: That's a beautiful way to put it, and I thank you for it. You know, when you're doing it, you're not conscious that you're bonding, but obviously, that's what you're doing, and it was certainly part of our survival, I would agree with that.

REFLECTIONS

o We're fortunate to be able to talk to people who have lived through historic events, especially if they've lived through events that have had a major impact on humanity, like Dr. Titze. Have you had any experiences in your life when singing played a role in how you processed real-world events? Whether celebration or trauma? How did singing have an impact on the way you felt?

o Does understanding how our survival instincts affect breathing and singing change your perspective on performing? In what ways?

o What are some of your favorite songs about courage or letting go of the past? You can find songs in religious music, opera, musical theater, traditional and folk music, classic rock, pop, R&B, hip-hop, and more!

LESSON ROUTINE A

Beginners: Use this plan for a minimum of two weeks.
Intermediate/Advanced: Use this plan for minimum one week.
All singers can use this plan as needed, for the rest of your life.

Like cutting and polishing a rough diamond, the scales and words I use with each singer depend on their unique voice and vocal habits. On your own, you have to rely on your powers to tactilize, audicize, and visualize. You can choose the scales you feel are the most comfortable. Avoid following "rules"—it's normal that each person has their own needs and reactions. Over time, you become aware of which exercises bring you results, so you can easily sing from low to high in one voice with even, medium volume and consistent contact. And, don't forget to have fun.

Begin by doing five to ten minutes of your favorite posture and respiration exercise from chapter 5. The breathing in these exercise stretches and relaxes the muscles of your body so you don't have to focus on it when you're singing.

VOICE TRAINING ROUTINE

Refer to the following scale series and remember to TAV:

2.1 Five-tone scale on lip rolls
2.3 Five-tone scale on *buh* and *bagh*
3.1 Triad with repeating octave on *goo* in a "hooty" voice, then *gee* in a "woofy" voice
3.2 Your upper voice using the "woofy" voice
3.3 Descending five-tone scale on *goo* or *new* in a "woofy" or "hooty" voice
3.4 Triad without consonants—use the *ee* or *oo* series of vowels
4.1 Octave-and-a-half arpeggio on lip rolls, then on *goo* and *gee*

LISTENING TRAINING

Listening to great singers provides you with a model for a voice that can move easily from low to high, with clear vowels and consistent contact, no matter what style of music you sing.

1. Listen to the entire song recommended below.

2. Print the lyrics, text or score.

3. Write any changes in dynamics, vowels, or tone on the printed page.

4. Go back and listen to the "money" notes, large intervals, or the chorus of each song.

5. Write which vowels and dynamics you hear on these sections of the song.

Female Contemporary and Musical Theater

Eva Cassidy, "True Colors"
Kelly Clarkson, "Because of You"
Jesse J, "Who You Are"
Sarah Vaughan, "Send in the Clowns"
"A Change in Me," from the musical *Beauty and the Beast*

Male Contemporary and Musical Theater

Beatles, "Yesterday"
Luther Vandross, "Knocks Me Off My Feet"
"Empty Chairs at Empty Tables," from the musical *Les Misérables*

Female Classical/Art Music

Montserrat Caballé (soprano), choose from *24 Italian Art Songs*, "Tu lo sai"
Marilyn Horne (mezzo-soprano), "Simple Gifts," arranged by Aaron Copland.

Male Classical/Art Songs

Thomas Hampson, "Shenandoah"
Luciano Pavarotti, "Una furtiva lagrima"

SONGS FOR YOU TO SING

Now, you can practice the skills you've learned in a new situation—music! Choose a song from the preceding list. You can even choose one from a genre you don't typically sing. Can you apply the training to music?

1. Print the lyrics/text to the song.

2. Read the words out loud. Find the meaning or translation of every word.

3. Circle the words that are the most interesting to you.

4. Circle the words that convey the main message of the song.

5. Listen to the song on a recording or play it on an instrument.

6. Circle words that you think are the most expressive.

7. Write the vowel sounds on the important words.

8. Learn the song using lip rolls instead of words.

9. Repeat any difficult sections, making sure you are TAV.

10. Sing the song using a vowel, consonant, or sound that will help you sing the difficult areas. Do you need to use the dopey dog voice, the hooty voice, or the witchy voice? Manage dynamics so you don't automatically sing louder on higher notes.

11. Sing the song with words.

Chart Your Experience

Answer yes, no, or don't know.

AFTER SINGING		AFTER RECORDING
_____	The tone suddenly changed at the higher notes.	_____
_____	I felt uncomfortable on the higher notes.	_____
_____	Tone was very quiet on the lower notes.	_____
_____	Inhale was calm without any gasping.	_____
_____	Tone sounds consistent without sudden changes.	_____
_____	Consonants feel easy and sound clear.	_____
_____	The dynamics are easy to manage.	_____
_____	The song felt easy to sing.	_____

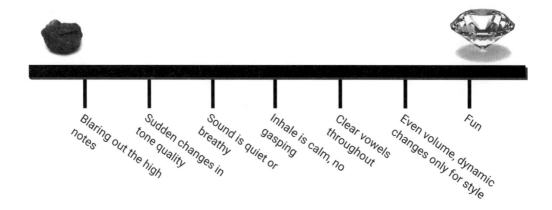

Blaring out the high notes | Sudden changes in tone quality | Sound is quiet or breathy | Inhale is calm, no gasping | Clear vowels throughout | Even volume, dynamic changes only for style | Fun

COACHING TIP

Try singing the song while walking backward to help maintain posture and engage your sensory system. Walk to the beat of the music!

Record and ask a buddy to listen. Chart your experience again.

REFLECTIONS

- How did you physically feel singing the song?

- Which tools helped you? Even volume? Consistent tone?

- Which parts of the song didn't work?

- What would you like to change about the way you sing the song? Can you choose a tool that will help you make that change?

- Which exercises would help you make the change?

PART II

How to Develop Mastery

6

REFINE RESONANCE

Prism: a transparent glass or plastic object that separates white light
that passes through it into different colours.

—*Cambridge English Dictionary*

You've been sorting and categorizing many small gems in the previous chapters. You've seen how singing is a motor skill, like learning to ride a bicycle or use chopsticks. Learning new motor skills requires that you intentionally direct your attention toward your senses; then you can practice, rest, and apply your skills to new situations until you develop mastery. Learning to direct your attention may be challenging, but when you have the right tools, and the courage to explore beyond your current experience, you can develop a free, expressive voice with the power and flexibility to sing a wide range of music, sharing your message with your listeners for the rest of your life.

You may still be struggling to sing the exercises and songs without reaching or pulling: maybe the vowels aren't clear yet, or you're still anxious about how your voice sounds or feels. But just as diamonds are formed under intense heat and pressure, your voice will be formed from your intense attention, practice, rest, and experience. Take time to record your singing, and notice changes you see, feel, and hear. What do you like? What do you dislike? What feels easy? What feels uncomfortable?

One of the compelling qualities of a diamond is how it disperses white light into many colors; diamonds are prisms. Did you know that your voice is like a prism, capable of dispersing many "colors"? In sound, "colors" refers to our perception of the tone quality. Usually, we want singing to include many colors—that is, frequencies occurring at optimum amplitude (volume), although sometimes the expression of the music and lyrics creates a tone with fewer colors, like expressing sighing, crying, yelling out in a dramatic moment, or rapping.

When you hear a breathy tone, or a power yell, or a clear, ringing tone—the harmonics and frequencies, the parts of the sound, are occurring in different amplitudes. We perceive changes in amplitude when frequencies and harmonic align (See chapter 3, page 57). Singers naturally develop a sense of managing the frequencies and harmonics without being aware of it, but you can also learn to audicize these properties, creating the resonance you want for songs. Your voice's ability to disperse many colors is one of the most effective ways your singing can become compelling for your listeners. Singing parts of your range with only one quality or volume doesn't allow you many choices for expression, or balancing with the other instruments. When you pay attention to how you're forming vowels, you will hear the tone quality of your singing change and become more resonant.

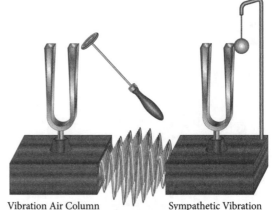

Vibration Air Column   Sympathetic Vibration
Sound Waves

The sound we hear increases when the frequency of sound waves is duplicated, or multiplied. These tuning forks are set to the same frequency. When the first one is hit with the mallet, the second one also vibrates (sympathetic vibrations). You can see it happen because the vibrations make the ball move. You can set the frequencies in the sound waves of your voice by balancing air and the muscles of your voice with the vowel, the amount of touch you use when you start the tone, and the amount of contact you maintain. This is how you get power and intensity in your singing. Audicizing and tactilizing before and during your singing allows your brain to collect the sensory information and make the necessary adjustments so you can line up frequencies and harmonics in a way that's effective for your style of music. The following scales help you focus on managing resonance.

6.1 SCALE SERIES
Finding Resonance

This is another example of a SOVT. Like the other examples, this will relax the muscles of your voice, train you to balance air and voice, and raise your awareness of resonance. Many singers use this exercise to rest or recover from oversinging or to prepare for performing, rehearsing, or recording.

1. Place your tongue between your lips, just slightly outside your mouth.

2. With your lips closed over your tongue, hum on one note. "Mm-hmm, good"

3. On the next page, sing *m* on each note, but avoid making a vowel. Open each *m* only very quickly. Do you feel your lips vibrating? Avoid large inhales. Do you feel loose and relaxed? If your lips don't vibrate, stay on the lower pitches and exhale evenly while singing until you feel vibration.

GOALS

- Lips vibrating, feel the buzz.

- Clear intonation, no "pitchy" tones.

- Only sing as high as you can keep the intonation clear while feeling the vibration. If you don't feel vibration in your lips, sing on a lower note.

SINGING A SENTENCE ON ONE NOTE

You can continue the chanting on one note with a sentence to get closer to real singing. I didn't write this sentence. But it has great vowels and consonants.

1. Use the same scale, chant on each note "My mom made me marmalade" instead of individual *m*'s.

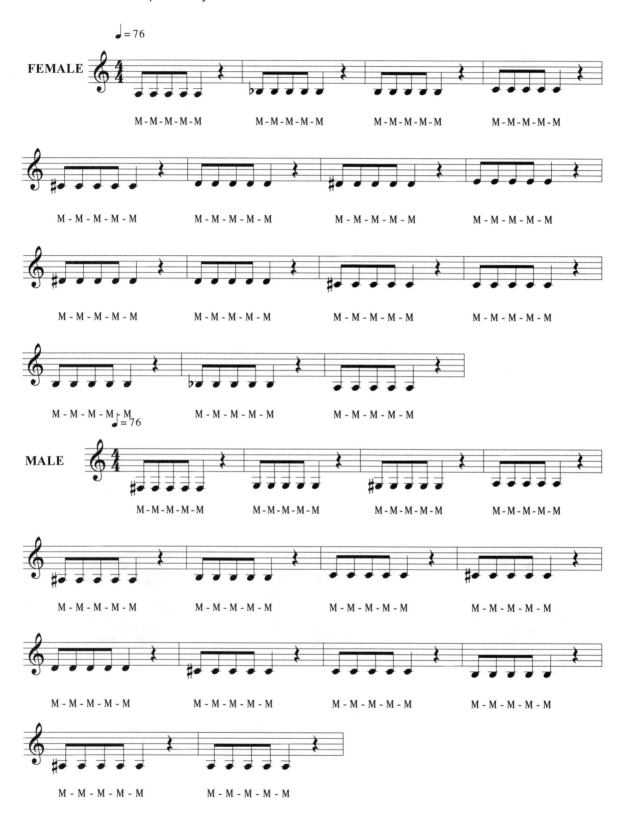

2. Keep the air moving through the *mm*; avoid allowing the *mm* to stop your singing.

3. Feel every vibration on your lips.

Chart Your Experience

Answer yes, no, or don't know.

AFTER SINGING		AFTER RECORDING
_____	My lips don't vibrate.	_____
_____	My lips vibrate sometimes.	_____
_____	It sounds like the intonation is "shaky."	_____
_____	I feel "thick" in the back of my throat.	_____
_____	My lips and face feel "buzzy."	_____
_____	Volume is even and easy.	_____

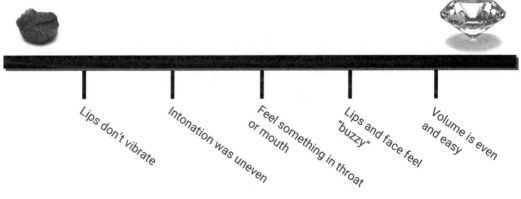

Lips don't vibrate — Intonation was uneven — Feel something in throat or mouth — Lips and face feel "buzzy" — Volume is even and easy

COACHING TIP

If your lips don't vibrate, just repeat singing on the lower pitches until you feel your lips vibrating consistently. If your lips stop vibrating during the note, focus on your upper lip.

Record on audio or video. Chart your experiences again.

6.2 SCALE SERIES
Octave-and-a-Half Arpeggio

Choose the scale for your voice type. Play the scale on your piano or keyboard, or listen to the audio file. Sing the scale on *muhm*.

To be sure that you're not adding tension, extend your tongue outside your mouth so that it's lying flat past your bottom lip, like your tongue is asleep. Soft, not stretching, not pointy. On every note, your lips touch your tongue (like your lips are "biting your tongue").

GOALS

o Make sure you're beginning the scale in your "talking voice." This is a neutral, relaxed, casual speaking tone. Try speaking *rum-tum-tum* a few times before you start singing.

o The end of the scale should have the same volume as the beginning.

o Avoid changing to *mahm* during the scale. If you can't maintain the vowel, stop singing, go back, and reassess.

o Relax the muscles in your torso between scales. Can you keep the vowel *uh*? Are you singing louder at the top? Try reducing volume to stay even.

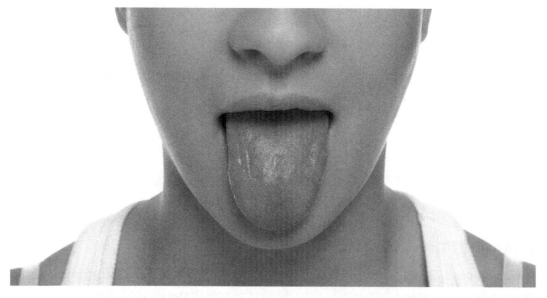

This is a nice, relaxed tongue resting between her lips. Can you sing with your tongue like this? You have to open your mouth to sing *muhm*, but your tongue can stay resting like this the whole scale!

Chart Your Experience

Answer yes, no, or don't know.

AFTER SINGING		AFTER RECORDING
_____	Unconsciously changed the vowel to *ah* during the scale.	_____
_____	Volume increased as the scale went up.	_____
_____	Volume decreased at the bottom of the scale.	_____
_____	My tongue can't stay extended during singing.	_____
_____	Volume decreased as the scale went up.	_____
_____	Contact was consistent throughout.	_____
_____	I felt a strong sense of the rhythm.	_____
_____	I sang a higher range than I usually do, and it was easy.	_____

Vowel became ah instead of uh — Volume increased during scale — Tongue is not flat — Quiet on the lower notes — Volume was even — Vowel was even — I felt the beat

DEBRIEF

If your larynx is relaxed, this should feel easy but engaged and resonant. If you get louder during the scale, you may be changing the vowel to *agh*, as in the English word *apple*. This is much more difficult, you'll have less control over the tone and your larynx will rise with the pitches.

COACHING TIP

You can try this exercise with a more "narrow" vowel as you ascend the scale. Begin the scale on *muhm* and change during the scale to *möm*, like the English word *good* (IPA= mʊm)

Record yourself. Chart your experience again.

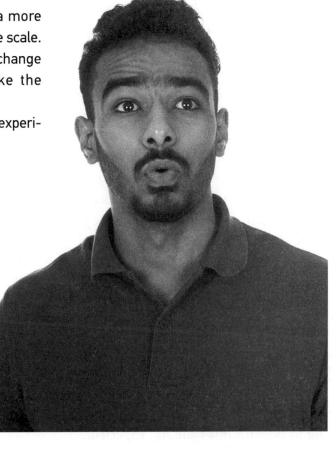

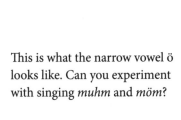

This is what the narrow vowel ö looks like. Can you experiment with singing *muhm* and *möm*?

In chapters 1 and 2, you saw that learning to sing is a complex neurological process that forms new neural connections between sections of the brain. This helps you approach your training with clarity. Similar to the way you learn to ride a bicycle or use chopsticks, you can learn to sing.

You've been working on forming new neural connections when you *tactilize*, *audicize* and *visualize*. If you're hitting any roadblocks, there may be a very concrete reason: you may have an imbalance between your *internal* and *external* focus.

Bodies function with different ways of focusing. When your focus is internal, your attention is directed to movements as your mind senses them inside your body, like inside your vocal tract or your lungs. External focus occurs when your mind senses movement outside your body, such as the effects your movements are having on the environment.[2]

Balance between internal and external focus creates the perfect conditions for motor learning and performance. Imagine trying to ride a bicycle while focusing solely on the feeling of your foot on the pedals. You would probably fall over! That's internal focus. Feeling the forces of gravity, weight, and air pressure—external focus—is how we learn to balance with only two thin wheels touching the ground. Your *experience* from internal and external focus teaches you how to ride a bicycle. Scuba diving works the same way. Just like singing, you get the information and instructions, watch someone do it (watch fish because they are really good at it), then try it, using a balance between internal focus and external focus to feel the sensation of breathing against the water and current. Soon it becomes automatic, like riding a bicycle. That's what you're learning to do with this training. *Experience* and balance the sensations of vowels, air, vibration, words, until singing becomes automatic.

You may have already had many times when you were singing and your voice "just worked"—or you felt that "when I get out of my head, I can just sing." When you have the information and training and the right balance between internal and external focus, it becomes automatic.

How do you know if your focus is internal or external? Your focus is probably too internal if

- you're singing with closed eyes very often; or
- you feel "stuck" in a habit, like reaching for an upper note, breathy singing, or singing with a raised larynx.

You can develop external focus by

- looking at something while singing. Is there a picture on the wall? An exit sign at the back of the theater? A nice view out the window? Really look at the details while you're singing;
- **TAV**
- moving to the beat while singing— tap your foot, or tap your hand on your hip.

The elephant balances internal and external focus too!

Do you remember the dopey dog? Can you audicize the dopey voice it might have? Can you think of other voices that may sound low and open like this? Santa Claus? Tarzan?

In Conversation with Tara Stadelman-Cohen

There are several types of medical professionals who work with singers. Speech language pathologists are one type. An SLP is educated and trained in speech and voice function, as well as clinical applications to help people who are ill, recovering from surgery, or just experiencing tired voices. So, in this interview, you will hear some facts directly from a professional, Tara Stadelman-Cohen, senior voice rehabilitation specialist and singing health specialist, at the Center for Laryngeal Surgery and Voice Rehabilitation at the Massachusetts General Hospital in Boston. Talking to singers and artists can be more fun than talking to an SLP, but sometimes a little direct information clarifies your concept of how to sing and how to direct your focus.

LINDA: When did you discover you were interested in voice, singing, and working with singers?

TARA: I was very active in music growing up, leading me to a get a bachelor's degree in music. I performed and taught voice before realizing that I desired greater knowledge in vocal physiology. After obtaining a master's degree in communicative disorders and becoming an SLP, I realized that a clinical specialization in the professional voice was ideal as it combined my two areas of study.

LINDA: Do you sing?

TARA: I sing daily as I need my instrument to be ready for patient demonstration. I have sung professionally, but the past few years have included a lot of singing children's songs to my six-year-old son—my most important audience!

LINDA: Could you say what is the most common problem you see with singers, in general?

TARA: A problem I frequently address is vocal fatigue. This can co-occur with nodules, or muscle tension dysphonia. Fatigue of voice can be common in the developing singer through the elite professional. Mild, intermittent fatigue can be normal, but if frequent or extended recovery is necessary, then it is problematic and should be assessed.

LINDA: Could you comment on the physical benefit of phonating with the tongue slightly extended to rest on the bottom lip, lying flat and relaxed, for an exercise?

TARA: I don't know of any study addressing isolated tongue extension, although that doesn't mean it isn't effective. At a minimum, this movement potentially increases a singer's awareness of an altered tongue position and muscle engagement, in addition to eliciting a different sensation of how air proceeds over the tongue.

LINDA: Could you comment on the use of one-note "chanting" on *mm* and the use of other SOVTs?

TARA: One-note chanting is a type of SOVT similar to the Accent Method of voice therapy. This approach may be beneficial for many reasons. First, there is the potential for reducing inefficient, habitual patterns associated with going from speech to song. Then, there is a connection of appropriate resonance with a rhythmic focus, which may allow a singer to employ more of a movement-based strategy. Also, there may be reduced complexity, so the singer may find it easier to subsequently reduce excessive muscle engagement.

The premise of SOVTs is to improve vocal economy, but not all SOVTs produce the same result. There can be differences in oral pressure and airflow across the vocal folds, the closed quotient, length of vocal tract, differing resistance [e.g., drinking straw vs. cocktail straw], and differing widths of the pharynx [throat]. Also, there are differences when there is one [humming] versus two sources of vibration [lip/tongue trills]. For example, if you wish to decrease excessive vocal fold adduction [closure], lip/tongue trills may be best as they have been found to have the lowest closed quotient. If you wish to address vocal fold strength while still reducing vibrational forces of the vocal folds, a straw may be best.

If you tend to reach, pull or squeeze, then sing scales and musical phrases on lip or tongue rolls. If you tend to sing breathy, or have trouble getting sound on some areas of your voice, then sing though a straw.

LINDA: Could you give a general example of your protocol for treating a common issue like muscle tension dysphonia?

TARA: Treatments are patient centered. Therefore, no single approach would be appropriate for every singer's unique challenges. In the clinical setting I have resource to assess and treat singers, like video endoscopy, acoustic and aerodynamic testing, the singer's perception of difficulty and hands-on palpitation of the laryngeal position and neck musculature. Treatment can address biomechanical symmetry and overall movement efficiency, massage and manual therapy to reduce laryngeal tension or implantation of rehabilitative strategies to improve respiration, phonation, resonance, and articulation.

LINDA: Does the neuroscience of motor learning inform your work?

TARA: I'm cognizant of it when rehabilitating patients, but it's only a subset of what drives my treatment. I do vary the type and frequency of feedback to allow for self-exploration and assessment. Feedback is dependent on patient needs as everyone has different learning requirements. Feedback also depends on the complexity of the skill being learned. And we've all had singers who can achieve something one week and the skill appears lost or less refined the following week, which is a perfect example of motor performance versus motor learning.

LINDA: How do you consider singers' auditory feedback when designing clinical protocols?

TARA: I view auditory feedback as one modality from which to learn and solidify greater efficiency in voice production. As much as singers are told not to listen to themselves, it remains an important and necessary part of the feedback loop. Studies have indicated auditory feedback can affect pitch, loudness control, and vibrato. Similar to any other talent, some accuracy of a singer's feedback is innate, and some is a learned skill. Voice rehabilitation is more physiologically oriented, so I tend to stress kinesthetic awareness more than auditory, as that can have greater consistency from environment to environment.

Auditory feedback is quite dependent upon the acoustics of the room, and whether one is singing solos, versus in a group, for example. At times, it can be useful to interfere with auditory feedback, and clinically I may use masking via white noise input through headphones in order to remove a singer's ability to hear their production. Also, hearing their sound at a delayed rate can alter production to eventually achieve a more desired end product as the feedback loop and previously learned muscle patterns have been affected. In reality, we likely do best with a combination of visual, auditory, and kinesthetic feedback.

LINDA: What would you recommend to singers experiencing difficulty with their voice?

TARA: Daily variation in vocal function can be normal. Similar to any athlete, concerns can arise from extensive and complex uses that increase normal wear on ligaments, joints, muscles, and vocal fold mucosa [membranes]. Importantly, reduced vocal function or actual injury should not have an associated stigma regarding a singer's technical skill.

A singer knows his or her own instrument best and is often aware when something does not feel or sound right. It can be typical for voices to be affected for weeks following a cold, although difficulty in the *absence* of illness is what is usually of most concern. Extended changes in function may be initially discussed with a voice teacher or coach. If perceived difficulty lasts longer than ten to fourteen days, medical assessment from a laryngologist is warranted—or even sooner, if desired.

REFLECTIONS

o Both Dr. Ingo Titze and Tara Stadelman-Cohen began singing at an early age, but they were driven to explore the "why," studying the physiology and biomechanics of the voice after years of singing. Can you think of any reasons our human survival instincts could be playing a role in their motivations (besides landing a steady job!)?

o Tara says that her six-year-old son is her "most important audience." Every human culture and language has lullabies and songs for children. Even Tara, a medical professional, feels the intensity of the drive to sing for her son. Children can survive without hearing songs from their mothers, but studies have shown the importance of the emotional bond developed through singing. Why do you think singing to babies helps them thrive?

o Have you discovered which SOVT exercise produces the best results in your voice?

o Tara refers to "rehabilitative strategies to improve respiration, phonation, resonance, and articulation." Can you name the strategies in this book that address each of these?

o Tara refers to the problem of achieving something vocally one week and then "losing" it the next week. You're learning in this book that sensory memory is the solution to this problem. By directing your attention to your sensory input, then memorizing it, you can recall movements more frequently, making them become automatic. Can you think of any occasions where you were able to audicize and tactilize successfully while practicing or performing?

Injury and technique. What's the connection? Many people compare professional singers to athletes because singers are using an ordinary movement (singing) in an extraordinary way. More range, more dynamics, more hours, many different environments and foods—all these things put demands on the anatomy and physiology that exceed the intention of the evolutionary design. This causes more wear and tear, so it's not surprising that any voice could have an injury. But consider great singers throughout history, opera singers like Joan Sutherland, or contemporary singers like Elvis Presley, Michael Jackson, Stevie Wonder, Beyoncé, to name a few. They had extraordinarily demanding schedules and difficult lives, and yet didn't have vocal injury.

Just like everything else to do with human bodies, there is a genetic component. For example, some people can smoke cigarettes for decades and never get lung cancer, while others suffer terribly and die before their time. Of course, if you never smoke cigarettes, your chances of getting lung cancer are drastically lower than if you smoke. Even so, people who smoke can't really be blamed or punished for getting lung cancer. It's not their fault that the market produced a product that is addictive and full of carcinogens. People who smoke their first cigarette and later die from lung cancer didn't *choose* to get addicted. Marketing, social pressures, and tobacco product design create an optimal situation for people to get easily addicted, or at least habituated, to smoking.

A professional singer's lifestyle creates a similar dilemma. Going on tour and performing eight shows a week on Broadway are probably beyond the original design of our anatomy and physiology. But history has shown, many legendary singers perform for decades without vocal injury. (At this writing, Tony Bennett is completing a national concert tour at ninety-two years old.) There are several rock singers over seventy years old showing no signs of slowing down despite decades on the road and suffering all the risky behaviors their lifestyle demands.

Yet headlines frequently shout stories of vocal injuries in our most extraordinarily gifted performers. What has changed for today's artists? The driving force behind singers' injuries may be industry expectations. With potential for enormous profits, the industry frenetically seeks the next great sound, the next great personality—encouraging young voices to sing bigger and cultivate a unique "sound," regardless of the impact that "sound" may be having on the singer's body. Even in opera, young voices are expected to "go big or go home," without consideration for the singer's physical maturity or skill development. Singing in enormous venues while ill and exhausted can cause serious vocal fatigue and even injury in the strongest artist, but relentless expectations from the music industry may be the forces needlessly damaging singers' voices, minds, and bodies.

A singer who suffers injury to the voice is no more at fault than a smoker who contracts lung cancer. Though it may appear that the singer "did something wrong" to cause vocal injury, there are many forces behind the scenes: business people making decisions about the singer and the songs they should sing, producers and engineers using technology and making decisions about tone qualities in the studio, a team of managers and assistants on the road with performers making decisions (or not making them) about the singer's schedule every day. And all these people derive their income from the singer's voice and performing. Canceling shows or tours is very costly.

That's putting the weight of the world on two small ligaments inside the body of a human being. People behind the scenes have an enormous responsibility to these artists. They have responsibility to protect singers. Managers have to create a relationship with the artist that makes protecting the voice, mind, and body a priority so that the artist trusts their viewpoint and advice. Creating and protecting the illusion of a brand has to become secondary to protecting the artist.

Of course, a professional singing career is a business, but a business that depends on a human body must have a different focus than one that depends on human-made product. The team behind the singer has to support, protect, and defend the singer. The team must guard the singer from demands on their voice that are dangerous. To do that effectively, they have to direct their attention to the singer's voice, mind, and body, rather than to the brand, the singer's "sound," or the sound they wish to create in the studio. That doesn't mean the business of singing can't be extremely profitable and successful. It just means that an instrument that is flesh and blood has to have priority over everything else.

And that includes *how* the singer is encouraged to use his or her voice. Many singers throughout modern history have developed their unique sounds and brands without sacrificing their health and voices. Singers and their teams have to recognize that healthy singing doesn't prevent a singer from having a unique identity or creating an emotional bond with their audience. The idea of a certain vocal "sound" being more marketable or easier to "sell" has been manufactured by the music industry. *Communicating a message and sharing an emotional bond doesn't require a manufactured "sound."*

Many singers have learned this the hard way. Mick Jagger took up voice coaching after decades of touring. He told Virgin Radio in 2006, "Better late than never. I always tell these younger singers: 'I never used to do it either, but you should.' I was speaking to Joss Stone and I mean, you sing a lot: every night you are singing for hours and hours and your voice gets tired: like anything else, like running every night."[3]

7

WHAT ABOUT POWER?

"Great singing wraps you in a shroud of humanity."

—LB

In previous chapters, you've explored your voice to discover how to sing, rather than what to sing. And you've probably found at least a few things you'd like to change about how you sing, like dynamics, resonance, and the amount of physical effort you use. You also learned that singing is a motor skill, like eating with chopsticks, but the biomechanics of vocal anatomy, acoustic perceptions, and the auditory system make singing a very complex motor skill. You've learned you can become intentional about your singing by directing your focus and using your sensory memory to sing with more freedom. And you've seen that singing evolved as one of our survival instincts, to share emotional experiences, bond families and tribes, find a mate, and

heal. There is still evidence of this today in modern culture.

The exercises you've been practicing are developing the connection between the lower and upper ranges of your voice, so you can sing in a "mix," the smooth effortless type of singing that allows your entire voice to be free and resonant, with a full range of dynamics. This way of singing gives you more choices, so your voice can be fully expressive, not just on a few money notes or a small part of your range. Once you master this, you can go on to create the style you need for any genre, from opera to rock to R&B.

The next training will begin to enhance tone and increase power, so you can sing in a *strong mix* (See page 30). Before you practice the scales, let's prepare by reviewing concepts and general practice guidelines.

◆ ◆ ◆

There are two concepts that can help you resolve any lingering issues in your singing: release and contact. *Release* may be important for you if you can't sing through your full range without getting louder, and if you feel like you're reaching, pulling, or squeezing. To find out if you need more release, pay attention to the following signs:

1. Does the volume automatically increase when you ascend in the scale or sing higher pitches?
2. Do the vowels change as you ascend in the scale? Does *"oo"* as in *new* change to *oh* or *uh*? Does *ee* as in *eat* change to *ih*, like the English word *it*?
3. After singing higher pitches, is it difficult to maintain volume or clarity on lower pitches?
4. Do you feel "thick" or "tight" in your throat when you ascend the scale?
5. Do you feel like you reach a "ceiling" when you try to ascend the scale?
6. Are you unable to sing with vibrato?

If you answered "yes" to two or more of these questions, there's a good chance you need to work on *release*. Release allows the voice to move throughout your range without straining for pitches. Remember the vocal folds can change pitches and range without any help, other than TAV.

You don't have to feel like you're pulling up weight when you sing higher notes!

TAV

1. Does your voice lose tone suddenly, usually at the same pitch range?
2. Is your vibrato different at different parts of your range or on particular vowels?
3. Does your voice sound louder on narrow vowels like *oo* and *ee* compared to wide vowels like *ah* and *uh*?
4. Does your tone/sound get soft or drop off at the end of words or phrases?
5. Do you feel like sometimes your voice doesn't carry, or can't be heard?

If you answered "yes" to two or more of these questions, there's a good chance you need to work on developing consistent *contact.*

Contact may be important for you if you're having difficulty singing with clear, consistent tone. Good contact means singing that feels consistent and firm, with a feeling of compression, like pressing all the way down on a keyboard, or leaning into the resistance when playing a wind instrument. But consistent contact never feels uncomfortable, there's no feeling of pressure or squeezing. In other words, you may have insufficient contact if the sound of your voice becomes quieter or "breathy" in parts of your range, or if you have vibrato that is very fast or very slow. To find out if you need more contact, pay attention to the following signs:

Can you tactilize the feeling of a firm handshake? Your singing can have a very similar sensation.

Having trouble answering the questions? Watch or listen to a recording of your singing, invite your buddy. Can you find any of the sounds and behaviors described above?

COACHING TIP

It's possible to have difficulties with *both* release and contact, at different times or at different parts of your range! Refer to the guide on page 27–28 for areas of voice that may be causing you difficulty.

Review the following table to find tools and strategies for your challenges.

TOOLS AND STRATEGIES

If higher pitches feel like yelling or blowing too hard,

then, focus on the pronunciation. Sing a clear *ee* or *oo* vowel in the scales. Audicize the vowel you want to sing and stay focused. The sound may not be pretty at first, but as long as you have connection without reaching or yelling, you are on your way.

If higher pitches feel like falsetto,

then sing with a "moaning" voice or add vocal fry at the beginning of the tone— *a small amount at a quiet volume.*

If you feel your stomach tightening when you sing,

then 1) sing SOVT or 2) walk while you're singing or 3) bow when you going up a scale, or 4) do posture and respiration exercises.

If you feel tightness in your throat,

then use the *woofy* sound. Sing the octave and a half on *wee* or *woof* or sing *muhm* with your tongue extended out of your mouth, lying flat and loose.

If you're still gasping when you inhale,

then practice a scale series without inhaling at all! Remember your body knows how much air you need but you may have a habit that is functioning like a "reflex." You don't have to analyze the process; when you interrupt your habits your body will figure it out. **Have courage.**

> ## Change Your Reflex for Breathing
>
> After you finish singing a scale, wait before you inhale, "drop" the muscles in your torso, letting them completely relax, to allow your diaphragm to return to its natural resting position, see page 108 (this may be a very small sensation or may even be imperceptible at first) then start singing immediately without any preparation. You might feel like you didn't inhale, but in fact your lungs will have taken in air, just as they do all day long when you're not aware of it.

COACHING TIP

Take time to sing through these recommendations or sing a few of your favorite scales from previous chapters before practicing the next scales.

7.1 SCALE SERIES
Funny Sounds, or Pharyngeals

7.1A TRIAD WITH OCTAVE REPEAT ON *NEY*
7.1B OCTAVE-AND-A-HALF ARPEGGIO ON *NEY*

The following set of scales may be the ugliest sounds you'll ever sing but they may also become your favorite tools for keeping your voice in shape. The funny sounds will train you to use less effort to get more contact, more release, and more resonance.

Ney is pronounced like the English word *neighbor* (IPA= nɛi), but when you sing this exercise, rather than singing in your regular speaking voice, imagine the voice of an unhappy toddler refusing to do what they've been told, or a little cartoon voice. Practice saying *ney* in that voice. Keep your face, and the inside of your mouth, calm.

1. Choose the scale.

2. Listen or play it once before you sing.

3. Say *ney-ney-ney* like an unhappy child. *Audicize* the voice of a toddler complaining about going to bed too early.

GOAL

With the inside of your mouth relaxed, try to lean in on your voice, so you maintain the bratty, unhappy, tone quality throughout the scale. This challenges your ability to tactilize. Can you find a feeling of easy compression—leaning against air?

The feeling of vibration may be intense, but the feeling in your throat is loose, like an open hand, not tight, like a closed fist. To find the sensation of singing an ugly, funny, witchy sound, tactilize singing toward the tip of your nose, not toward your mouth. Is your rib cage going up when you inhale?

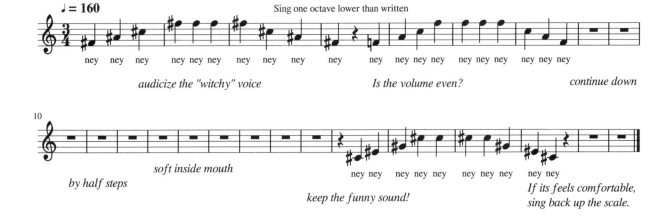

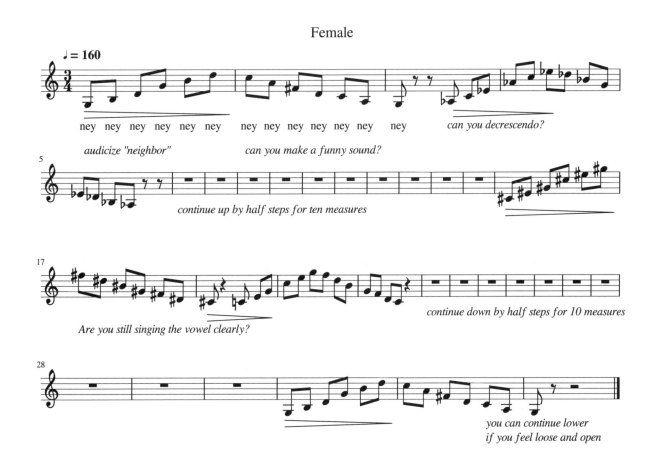

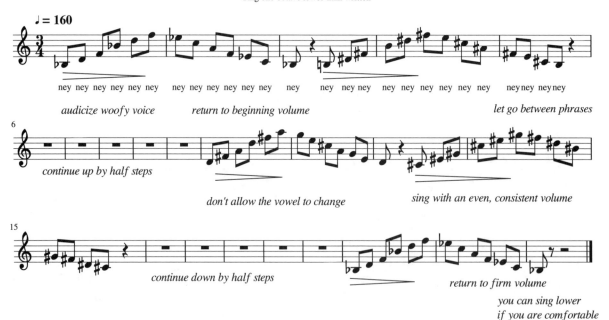

Chart Your Experience

Answer yes, no, or don't know.

AFTER SINGING		AFTER RECORDING
_____	Felt tight making the funny sound.	_____
_____	Couldn't maintain the sound through the scale.	_____
_____	Vowel changed to *nuh* in the upper notes.	_____
_____	Sound got quieter on the lower notes.	_____
_____	Couldn't feel the beat.	_____
_____	Sang louder as the scale went higher.	_____
_____	Scale felt easy.	_____
_____	Volume was even.	_____
_____	Breathing felt easy and calm without gasping.	_____

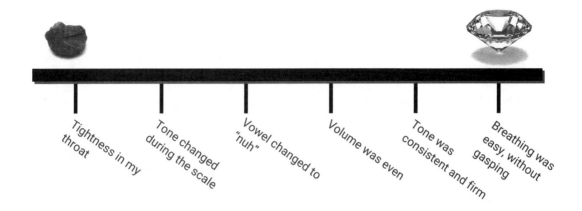

Tightness in my throat | Tone changed during the scale | Vowel changed to "nuh" | Volume was even | Tone was consistent and firm | Breathing was easy, without gasping

DEBRIEF

Did you inhale calmly, without a big preparation, without gasping? Could you avoid oversized inhales?

If you feel "thick" in your throat, reduce the volume and make the inside of your mouth passive. If you feel tight, wiggle your jaw a little while you're singing. Did you tactilize the correct touch for the beginning of the first note?

COACHING TIP

Is your *n* free? Training your tongue to move independently from your jaw will allow you to sing with less effort. Check your tongue's independence: Open your mouth with relaxed lips and hanging jaw. Without moving your jaw, raise the tip of your tongue to the roof of your mouth.

Can you make a clicking noise by flicking your tongue on off the roof of your mouth without moving your jaw?

With your mouth closed, use the tip of your tongue to trace your teeth. Put the tip of your tongue at the back, outside, top teeth and move your tongue around your mouth on the outside of your teeth, like tracing your teeth. Do the same for the top, inside, the bottom, outside, and the bottom, inside.

Record your singing. Invite your buddy to watch or listen. Chart your experiences again.

7.1C TRIAD WITH OCTAVE REPEAT ON *NAGH*

7.1D OCTAVE-AND-A-HALF ARPEGGIO ON *NAGH*

The next "funny" sound is singing on the vowel *agh*, found in the American English pronunciations of *at, cat, nasty*. "Look at that nasty cat" (no offense to cats).

- Choose the same scale as in the previous exercise but now sing with *nagh* (IPA= næ).

- Play or listen once before you sing.

- Say *nagh-nagh-nagh* like a cackling witch. Can you audicize her voice before you sing and during your singing? You may feel like the area behind your face is very open when you sing. Avoid feeling any pressure or effort in your mouth.

GOAL

These funny sounds will train you to sing with consistent contact, with more intensity, and without pulling or reaching. Continue the vowel clearly throughout the range, no matter what happens! You may feel a lot of vibration behind your face, and even between your ears.

Chart Your Experience

Answer yes, no, or don't know.

AFTER SINGING		AFTER RECORDING
_____	Felt tight making the funny sound.	_____
_____	Couldn't maintain the sound through the scale.	_____
_____	Vowel changed to *nuh* in the upper notes.	_____
_____	Sound got quieter on the lower notes.	_____
_____	Couldn't feel the beat.	_____
_____	Louder as the scale went higher.	_____
_____	Breathing felt easy and calm without gasping.	_____
_____	Scale felt so easy!	_____

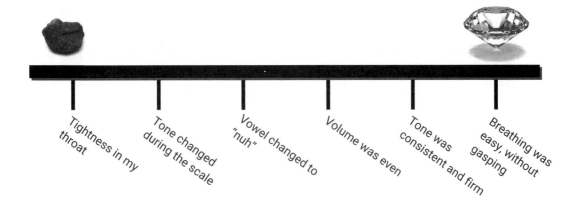

Tightness in my throat

Tone changed during the scale

Vowel changed to "nuh"

Volume was even

Tone was consistent and firm

Breathing was easy, without gasping

DEBRIEF

Did you inhale calmly, without gasping, without overpreparing?

If you feel "thick" in your throat, reduce the volume and make the inside of your mouth calm. If you feel tight, move your jaw a little, like chewing, while you're singing.

COACHING TIP

Play! If you're having trouble going through the scale, the reason may be tension in your mouth or tongue, so focus on the vowel. You have to stay in a "witchy" voice. Can you hear her cackling?

Record yourself singing the scale. Ask your buddy to watch or listen. Chart your experiences again.

COMMON QUESTIONS ABOUT PHARYNGEALS

"Why am I making an ugly sound?"

When you're making the ugly sounds, you're changing the sound by making the "tube" of your vocal tract narrow, creating faster airflow and lower air pressure. Imagine a flag hanging from a pole on a warm, sunny day. The sky is blue, the birds are singing, there's a soft breeze in the air. The flag gently waves to and fro, sometimes hanging flat, and other times lifted by a brief whiff of wind. The next day, the weather changes. A storm appears on the horizon bringing hurricane force winds. Before the dark clouds and rain appear, the wind begins tossing the flag. No longer relaxed and hanging casually on its pole, the flag is whipped into a frenzy, flapping quickly back and forth, the energy of its own movement keeping the flag aloft.

See what happens to the flag when the airflow speeds up? This is similar to what happens to your voice when the airflow moves faster. The sounds *ney* and *nagh* help you increase the speed because they narrow the tube. Try blowing through a large straw and then a narrow straw. Can you feel the difference? The airflow is faster in the narrow straw. Over time, you will be able to feel your voice resisting the airflow and pressure just like you feel it when singing through straws.

"Is this hurting my voice?"

No. But if you tighten the back of your tongue and reach for the upper ranges, you will be uncomfortable. This will tire your voice and ruin the intonation. If you maintain the vowel and volume, you will get the results you want.

"Am I going to sound like this when I sing?"

This is a temporary exercise to train coordination. Once you develop the ability to audicize the vowel and tone and tactilize these vowels, you may not have to continue this exercise. If you're a classical singer, you may only need to practice these for a short time. If you sing musical theater, R&B, pop, or rock, you may want to keep this exercise in your regular toolbox. Training your voice with these sounds won't make you sound like this when you sing unless you choose to do so.

"How do I get it loud?"

Increasing your volume is never a *direct* goal. Volume is an outcome. When you keep a clear vowel and consistent volume and consistent contact, the intensity of your singing increases with time—just like when you exercise your abdominals. Abdominal muscles don't appear immediately, you have to train them for a period of time and gradually build strength by increasing the workout. Singing is very similar. You will get immediate results from forming vowels and managing volume, but even greater results when you train, increasing the workout step by step over a period of time. But if you feel like you're not getting contact at all, reread the beginning of this chapter.

"Is this nasal singing?"

No, nasal singing isn't a sound you should use for training because it requires muscles that elevate the larynx. To practice, pinch your nose closed while you sing. If you sound like a duck, you are singing nasally. Visualize directing the air toward your mouth. Trying singing or speaking with your nose pinched closed without sounding like a duck. Practice a few times with pinching and not pinching your nose until you tactilize the difference. The exercise is training your perception of the velar port, the opening to the nasal passage, commonly called the soft palate.

"Is this belting?"

The funny sounds are a great way to boost the intensity of your singing quickly and without muscular effort. The word "belting" is used by many people in many different ways. Generally, people use "belting" to describe loud resonance or intensity in the first transition of your voice. Casting notices refer to "belt" when they are looking for a powerful singer. But the "how-to" for producing intense sound is taught in many different ways. The intensity of the pharyngeal sounds can be increased or decreased at will when you've developed mastery. For example, a Broadway singer may use a more intense pharyngeal than an opera singer, who may only begin with a funny sound to develop the coordination, but later change to less intensity, as in the singing of operatic tenors Nicolai Gedda and Beniamino Gigli.

◆ ◆ ◆

So, what exactly creates powerful singing? Powerful singing seems to have originated in Africa. Even today, we can hear singing used by indigenous peoples that is full of energy and intensity. But their bodies and throats don't exhibit the tension or problems we hear in Western singers trying to be loud. The only concrete documentation we have about how to sing powerfully begins in the Middle Ages. There are descriptions from the sixteenth and seventeeth centuries of castrati singers whose powerful, flexible, and dramatic voices drove their fans wild. The castrati, who first gained popularity in the mid-sixteenth century in Spain, and then in Italy, were castrated in their youth so they could keep their soprano voices throughout their lives. They could sing in the female range but with the lung capacity (energy source) and vocal tract size (resonating tube) of a man. This created a very powerful sound, and the castrati were widely popular until the beginning of the eighteenth century.[2]

Fortunately, today we have other methods to develop powerful voices! There are many singers born with the anatomy and physiology to produce a lot of volume, but just about any singer can learn to produce a powerful tone, even though the degree of power may vary from person to person. A very small person can have a very powerful voice, and a large person could have a lyrical, sweet voice, but generally, if you have a large chest and a large throat, you are likely to have capacity for greater amplitude.

There are two problems that come up most frequently when singers try to sing with power. Either the singer uses too much muscular effort, by reaching, pulling, or pressing muscles in the throat, neck, or voice, or the singer takes huge, labored breaths, followed by a pushy or squeezed exhale. Many times these problems are combined, which can create a "cause-and-effect" relationship. In any case, both problems can be resolved with balanced training that includes the voice, body, and mind. In terms of the mind, you may find it easier to TAV for powerful singing when you know a little bit about how it works.

Powerful singing is a mechanical and acoustic event that happens as a result of a balance between air and vocal fold coordination and the muscles and positions in the vocal tract. Although the vocal tract is basically a tube from the top of your vocal folds to the end of your lips, there are structures within it. The epiglottis is a small structure just above your voice that prevents food and drink from entering your voice and lungs, with a tiny resonating space because of its shape. Then, of course, you have a very large, complicated muscle, the tongue. It's composed of three internal muscle pairs that can change the shape and three external muscle pairs that can extend and retract it upward and downward. There is also the velar port that can open or close the passage to the nose. All these affect the acoustic intensity of your singing.[3] You've been learning and practicing how to coordinate all of these from the training in this book. While you've been singing these exercises, your body and mind have been learning how to manage all these components. It's helpful to remember that the vocal tract is not a one-piece, passive unit—the epiglottis, the glottis, the tongue, mouth, and lips are moving parts, not a static tube. Each area is made up of muscles, cartilage, or other tissues that you can form in a variety of ways. There are also some nooks and crannies where the sound waves can resonate. Conscious movements (such as making *oo* lips) and unconscious fine motor skills (such as the movements in your throat) are the craft of singing.

Managing the length and width of the vocal tract and its components, as you do when you form vowels or using voices like "woofy" "hooty" "cackling" or "moaning," has a dramatic impact on the intensity of the sound. This is most noticeable when you train funny sounds, like the *ney* or *nagh*, but you can hear it and feel it even on lighter sounds.

Recently, I was coaching an advanced high school choir visiting Boston to perform contemporary Christian a cappella choir music. They were highly trained, excellent musicians with a lovely sound. The choir director asked me in advance if I could address the problem of low volume in the alto section. When I worked with the choir, I heard almost everyone singing with low intensity. The sound was pretty, but dull, lacking the resonance that makes a choir shake the walls of a concert hall. But it was more noticeable in the altos because of the lower range. These young women hadn't yet developed consistent contact in their lower voices. After working with everyone on clear vowel production and shaping the musical phrase, I asked the altos to sing alone. Most of the song was on the vowel *oo*, which is by no means a loud vowel, but they could hardly be heard at all! We worked on their vowels, paying particular attention to pursing the lips in a whistle-shape, while at the same time, shaping the musical phrase. We practiced it twice, and suddenly the sound dramatically increased, so much that heads turned and gasps were heard from the non-singing choir members and the director. They were only singing an *oo* vowel, but the intensity increased because changing the shape of the vocal tract (lips, tongue, and laryngeal position) increased contact.

You can do the same thing. And when you apply these principles to the funny sounds and the vibrato exercise (see following), you can dramatically increase the power of your voice without reaching, blowing huge amounts of air, losing tone, or getting vocally fatigued.

INTRODUCTION TO VIBRATO

Vibrato is an important quality of your singing because it's a naturally occurring phenomenon and part of human vocal expression. Sometimes singers ask me how to "make" vibrato, or how they can control vibrato, but it's actually far less complicated than many singers believe. When you pluck a string that is held at both ends, like a string on an instrument or a rubber band stretched out between two hands, the string will vibrate. This is oscillation. The vocal folds are something like two ribbons held at the front end and back end, and when they're set in motion they will oscillate. (It's very important for the vocal folds to have vibrato because it's a time of rest.)

There are two things about vibrato that may be helpful for you. First, vibrato helps you communicate because it's expressive, and the type and style of the vibrato can change according to emotion. If you hear someone scream in fear, as in a horror movie, the sound produced generally doesn't have any vibrato. That's because tension is "holding" the vocal folds, preventing them from vibrating. We unconsciously understand this absence of vibrato as a particular emotional state. But if someone is crying or speaking when very sad, the voice may have a wide, shaky vibrato because the vocal folds are too loose, lacking the tautness they would need to vibrate evenly. Likewise, when you sing, vibrato sends an important part of the emotional message.

Understanding and practicing vibrato in your voice is also helpful because it can be considered a bellwether, a measure of how your voice is working overall. If you don't have any vibrato in your singing, or the vibrato is too "wide," like very loose string, or a table with an uneven leg, or too fast, like the sound of a bleating goat, it's a sign that the voice is out of balance—the airflow and muscle activity aren't coordinated.

If you haven't specifically considered your vibrato, you may not even hear what's happening. I trained an operatic soprano who was a recent graduate from a well-known, highly regarded conservatory. She had an undergraduate and a master's degree in vocal performance, and she'd sung several roles in school and preprofessional young artist programs. She had a good-sized lyric soprano voice with great warmth and expression, but her tone was very inconsistent, to the point that she often had intonation problems in parts of her voice. When I first heard her, the most dramatic characteristic of her voice was her vibrato. It was wide, almost wobbly, and inconsistent. It sounded like the vibrato of a sixty-year-old retired singer.

She was twenty-seven but her voice sounded wobbly and inconsistent because her vibrato was too wide. When I said her singing would be more consistent if she addressed the vibrato, she was stunned. She'd had almost fifteen years of voice training and coaching, along with two degrees, but no one had ever mentioned her vibrato. We worked on the following exercises, and in a few weeks, her entire voice balanced out and her singing became more flexible and more powerful. (Remember, she was an experienced singer; if you are a beginner, it may take longer for you.) Her prominent Boston vocal coach was very impressed with the changes in her voice. She went on to sing with another pre-professional program where she got considerably more attention than she had in previous experiences because her vibrato had improved the intensity of her voice and allowed her to be more expressive and musical.

You may already be singing with an effective, naturally occurring vibrato. In that case, you can still play with it in the following exercises to develop the ability to add or remove it when you want. For example, in Broadway music, or other kinds of power singing, you may want to start a long note without vibrato and slowly introduce it. In R&B, rock music, and traditional songs, vibrato is often just on the ends of the phrase or sentence. You can easily learn to do all these things when you tactilize and audicize the sensation.

7.2 SCALE SERIES

Five-Tone Scale with Vibrato on Each Note

You will be able to do this exercise in all parts of your range, but you can begin with the easy range.

- Choose the scale for your voice type (See pages 18-19).

- Play the scale.

- TAV the vowel *oo* as in *google*.

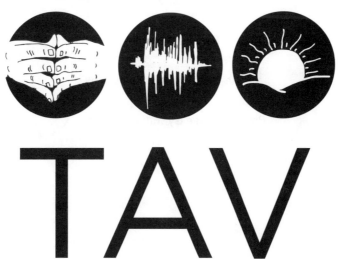

While singing, on the first note and last note, shake your hand as if you are trying to shake water off. Any movements you make with your hands usually has an effect on your vocal folds. The working theory for this cause and effect is that the area of the brain that is responsible for moving the vocal folds is very close to the area for hand and facial movement, and signals from them merge along the same pathways.[4]

GOALS

Maintain consistent *volume* and *contact* throughout the scale and throughout the range. Volume is especially important here. If you exhale too much air, your voice won't have vibrato and may be out of tune.

Avoid "making" vibrato in your throat. Continuously shake your hand while you're singing.

Chart Your Experience

Answer yes, no, or don't know.

AFTER SINGING		AFTER RECORDING
_____	Felt tight.	_____
_____	Couldn't hear/feel any vibrato.	_____
_____	Intonation was uneven.	_____
_____	Sound got quieter on lower notes.	_____
_____	Ran out of breath.	_____
_____	Vibrato was very fast or very slow.	_____
_____	Breathing felt easy without gasping.	_____

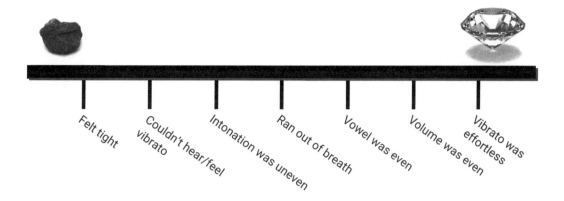

Felt tight

Couldn't hear/feel vibrato

Intonation was uneven

Ran out of breath

Vowel was even

Volume was even

Vibrato was effortless

DEBRIEF

Patience. This isn't an easy exercise. Managing volume is the key to success. If you're an experienced singer, you may find it easy at first, but to really maintain good intonation, you'll have to manage your volume carefully. Continuously shake your hand while singing.

COACHING TIP

If you are uncomfortable, having trouble with intonation, or don't feel like there's any vibrato, check how you *begin* the scale. Start the first note with a relaxed consonant and a gentle touch, like a feather falling on a pillow. The first note should feel *buoyant*. During the scale, be sure to audicize the vowel while you're singing the scale. If you feel comfortable, try the scale in a higher part of your range

Record your singing. Invite your buddy to listen. Chart your experiences again.

8

BROADEN PERSPECTIVE

I just want people to take a step back, take a deep breath and actually look at something with a different perspective.

—Brian McKnight, American R&B singer-songwriter, arranger, producer, and musician

In the previous chapters, you've learned many scales, routines, and concepts to discover how to use your voice. You've heightened your sensory awareness and memory so you can tactilize, audicize, and visualize. New neural networks are forming, slowly moving over to long-term memory storage so you can automate your ability to sing with freedom, flexibility, and power. But as an artist you also need freedom, flexibility, and power in your mind.

Becoming an artist means discovering the ability to do what you intend to do without blocks or limitations. You may not be aware that you have any blocks, or you may be plagued by feelings that distract you from your work. Everyone has some

degree of stress, anxiety, worry, or fear—it's part of what makes us human. But you can't become an intentional singer if you're veering off course or allowing distractions to limit your skills and creativity. You are unique, and you have your own unique patterns, habits, attitudes, and beliefs. Just like discovering your voice and how to use it, you can learn tools and strategies to discover what's making you veer off course. Begin by expanding your perspective. There are many ways to do this, but there's nothing like meeting someone who got impaled by a tree!

In my mid-twenties, I was living in Europe pursuing my passion for singing. I had been living as an expatriate for a few years, visiting the Vienna State Opera five nights a week and studying with a wonderful opera coach, but I felt like I was getting stuck. I wasn't moving forward as fast as I imagined I should be. In the summer, I returned to the United States for a visit. My mother and I took a trip to Tallahassee, Florida, to visit my brother, who was a busy trauma surgeon. When we arrived at the small airport, my brother met us at the gate. As we began whisking our roller bags through the airport hallways, friendly greetings hailed from every direction, "Hello, Dr. Balliro." It seemed we couldn't walk more than ten seconds without someone waving to my brother. Then a slightly built older man with wisps of graying, blond hair loudly called out an enthusiastic "Dr. Balliro!" waving emphatically, with a broad, infectious smile. My brother stopped in his tracks, wide-eyed and grinning from ear to ear. He briskly walked over to the man and shook his hand vigorously and they began a lively chat. When my brother returned to where my mother and I were waiting, he was beaming. He told us the following story.

"I was called into the ER one night for a logging accident. The place was in chaos, with nurses and attendants scurrying around anxiously wringing their hands, some of them quietly crying. The patient was alone behind a screen. Everyone was afraid to talk to him. I went behind the screen and saw this small guy lying on the gurney with a large tree trunk protruding from his stomach. No kidding, this guy had a tree trunk in his stomach." Staying calm amid the panic around him, my brother just looked the man in the eye and said, "Good afternoon, Mr. Smith. What's the problem today?" My brother was known for his unusual sense of humor. But underneath the humor, he was trying to change the atmosphere and calm the patient because the panicked doctors and nurses were only making the situation worse.

The patient was a logger. He had been out working with a logging crew cutting down trees when a large tree unexpectedly fell and *impaled* him. Despite having a tree through his body, he was quite alive, conscious and talking. His crew somehow had the presence of mind to cut the tree at both ends, leaving the stump stuck in his stomach so he wouldn't bleed out. They carried him to a logging truck and drove it down the long dirt road through the woods to the hospital. The logger was awake and talking the entire journey. At the ER, the shock and horror of the accident created chaos, but my brother just stayed cool, talked to the man in a calm voice, got him into surgery, removed the tree trunk, stitched him up, and sent him off to a specialty hospital for bowel surgery. A few years later, here he was, walking around at the airport in Tallahassee happily waving at us.

So, while I was off in Europe working on jaw tension and worrying about whether my high notes were consistent enough to audition for a particular conductor, my brother was operating on a man who had been impaled by a tree. This certainly helped me with perspective.

Singing is an important part of life, society, and humanity, but my problems were tiny compared to facing someone who has a tree stump in their stomach.

I've told this story to several of my students when they've been feeling stuck, as if there's something keeping them from moving forward. One time, I told the story to a Berklee student who had been studying with me for three years. She is a very talented singer, pianist, and arranger, and the story immediately sharpened her perspective. She had been stalling on establishing her public presence as a musician. She was worried she wasn't ready to blast her music out to the world. The idea of a website, social media, and building a fan base were bouncing around in her mind, but "gremlins" inside her head were warning her of all the imaginary dangers: she wasn't ready, she wasn't good enough, maybe she should wait until she had a perfect song. Although she was a talented, highly skilled, and intelligent young artist and she knew the words in her imagination weren't true, she didn't have the tools to ignore them and form a calm, focused mind.

When I told her the story, we both reached the end almost in tears. And she was so moved that she began to think about her life differently. She's out in the music world now, performing, recording, and living her passion. She said she thought about the story many times, and it gave her the perspective she needed to create a realistic vision of her career, rather than a twisted apparition of her worst fears.

So even though you're working hard to learn how to sing, you need to have a calm, focused mind to become a great singer. Perspective is the first step. We all need to keep a broad perspective in our lives, but artists especially need it. There are fans and critics everywhere—among your family, friends, audition juries, producers, or colleagues. If you're surrounded by people who think you can do no wrong (not helpful) or if you have a few constant critics (harmful), perspective can help you stay focused so you can keep your voice in condition and stay in the moment of the music.

Every performer, artist, and musician I know has a personal strategy to keep a calm, focused mind. I practiced yoga meditation when I was performing regularly, and now I use insight meditation. I work with a singer who practices Transcendental Meditation. I know singers who practice prayer, meditation, or Buddhism, and some who just take long walks to relax and stay focused. Lady Gaga tells a story about meeting George W. Bush. She told him she had been to his church. He said, "But my church is Methodist, aren't you Roman Catholic?" She said it was the day of her Super Bowl performance; she didn't care what church it was, she just needed Jesus.[1]

Practicing meditation or prayer, taking a walk in the woods, or just sitting and being quiet for a while allows you to keep your perspective about your voice, your singing, and even other important areas of your life. The following exercise will clarify your perspective, helping you form and maintain a calm, focused mind.

8.1 EXERCISE
Expanding Your Perspective

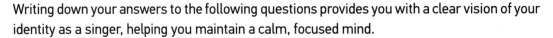

Writing down your answers to the following questions provides you with a clear vision of your identity as a singer, helping you maintain a calm, focused mind.

- List two unique qualities about your voice. Is there something you always hear from your friends, family, or fans about your voice? Beautiful? Powerful? Flexible? Be specific. _____

- List two ways you enjoy demonstrating these qualities when you sing. Any particular songs? Improvisation? Range? Slow? Fast? _____

- Describe a perfect performance. Where are you? What are you singing? What kind of audience is there? Are you singing with anyone else? What does it feel like?

  _____

- Combine your answers from all the questions into one single sentence. The unique qualities of my voice are _____, and I enjoy demonstrating them with _____ and performing at _____."

(Adapted from the work of Arnold Patent)

MINDFULNESS OR STAYING IN THE MOMENT

In previous chapters you have experienced that being aware and focused makes learning to sing easier and more enjoyable. Just as you have practiced tactilizing, audicizing, and visualizing, you can practice focusing your attention to develop a calm, focused mind.

Some of the greatest performers I have seen and worked with appear very calm because they can freely focus their attention, without thoughts or emotion distracting them. If your mind wanders to a thought or a negative image for even a nanosecond, your performance is negatively affected. Or, if there is constant chatter in your mind, you are distracted by things that are not real. Learning to focus your attention is often called *mindfulness*—the ability to "stay in the moment." When you're aware of your environment your mind becomes calm and it's possible to focus on whatever you want.[2]

This tendency toward mental chatter is left over from our survival instincts. If you are in immediate danger and you need to escape, you need this ability to quickly run through many scenarios in your mind. But we don't need this ability on a daily basis and, like other instinctive responses, you can develop the skill to manage it. There are many methods and approaches to mindfulness, or developing your ability to stay in the moment. You can have fun exploring options and strategies to find your favorite.

Not sure where to begin? Just start in your daily life. Practice mindfulness or a kind of focus and meditation in your daily routine. When you are walking down the street, choose something to look at and focus your attention so that you really look at the details. Do you see a tree? Focus on the shape, color, and size. Is it old? Can you see details on the bark, the leaves? Or maybe you are washing dishes. Can you focus your mind on the water? How does it run off the dish? Is it hot or warm? Is it soapy? Does is feel slippery or gooey? Does the running water sound like "shooosh" or "chug"? You'll see that when you stop to focus on small, specific details, you are already developing a calm, focused mind. Then you can use the same strategy in your practicing, rehearsing, and performing.

In Conversation with Mike Gordon

I have a confession to make. There are a lot of things I don't know. During the 1990s and early 2000s, I was living in Vienna working on my repertoire and vocal technique, auditioning, and performing. I was spending all my time on buses and trains and in tiny hotels, focused on maintaining my health and voice. So I missed the happenings in the United States during that time. That's why, in June 2012, when I got a voicemail from a woman saying she was calling for Mike Gordon from the band Phish, I was a bit in the dark. I had to play the voicemail a few times to make sure I'd heard the name correctly. I had *heard* of Phish. I knew they were an established band of serious musicians who played good music, and they'd been around for a long time. But I didn't quite know what they were—was it jazz, rock? And which one in the band was Mike Gordon? I had to go to Wikipedia and YouTube to figure it out. (Even then, it was months before I understood the phenomenon of Phish, if it *can* be understood.) Since Phish was just about to start the summer tour for 2012, we began working immediately. I sent Mike to see Dr. Stephen Zeitels in Boston before we began serious study, since every performing singer who is making a change in their voice should get a doctor's exam first. Then, Mike and I began dissecting his singing habits, unearthing gems he didn't know were there, finding his strengths, and developing a process that would allow him to sing easily while playing the bass. Discoveries about his voice and singing allowed him to become a more focused songwriter and a more confident performer. Now, the Mike Gordon Band, with Mike as lead singer, has come into its own, discovering a sound and feel that is incredibly creative and compelling. So, relax, kick back, clear your mind, and read about Mike Gordon's thoughts and experiences with singing. I'm sure you'll want to check out both his band and Phish if you don't already know them.

LINDA: You said that you wrote and recorded a song for Store 24 [the first convenience grocery store in the United States that was open twenty-four hours a day] with your friend. Is that your earliest singing experience?

MIKE GORDON: Yes, that must've been about 1973. Also, in Hebrew day school there was a lot of singing, although I was the one who didn't sing much with the class. But there were a lot of Hebrew prayers that were very evocative, and I had that half a day for seven years.

LINDA: But you didn't like to sing in those classes?

MIKE GORDON: I was just shy. But those melodies, they stick in my head, and they were very much a part of my being.

LINDA: Those melodies are incredible music—I coached a rabbi who was recording some prayers that had been lost—they were stunning. So, when you recorded this song for Store 24 when you were a child, what made you think of singing for that song rather than just playing an instrument?

MIKE GORDON: Um, well, just because we heard things on the radio and they were often sung and even commercials had jingles—so I think we wanted to be like that. I had been listening to a lot of music since I was born probably—there were a lot of Beatles albums being played, and Leonard Cohen, things like that, so there was definitely, between the Hebrew stuff and the Beatles stuff, there was a lot of singing around.

LINDA: OK, so you just sang it without thinking about it, but you were just a little kid, about eight? And the two of you came up with the lyrics?

MIKE GORDON: Yup, lyrics, melody, everything. But when we got to the recording studio, they had the backing track already made, so—

LINDA: When you heard it back, you said you went to hide in a corner?

MIKE GORDON: Yeah, I heard my own voice, and it didn't sound like what I thought it sounded like, and suddenly I was embarrassed.

LINDA: Did anyone say anything to you about your voice, or was that just your own reaction?

MIKE GORDON: I don't think anyone said anything, just my own reaction.

LINDA: One of the things we're discussing in this book is why people sing, and why they have such a judgmental reaction to their singing. The premise is that singing is part of our survival instincts, so if we don't sing well, there's an ancient response that we might lose our connection to our tribe or group.

MIKE GORDON: Right, that is a theory, but obviously you hear yourself in your head very differently than the way it comes out—and the recording quality is another thing . . .

LINDA: Mm-hmm.

MIKE GORDON: But the vibration through your head is bound to be somewhat deeper because of your skull vibrating—well, it depends on how you sing, I guess.

LINDA: Yeah, it depends. There was some research suggesting that the vibrations cause fluid in the brain to move around. If you think of a glass of water on top of a speaker, the water vibrates.

MIKE GORDON: Yeah (*laughs*).

LINDA: When you started singing with Phish—I found an old video of an interview with the four of you. Trey was talking about singing, and you said something about how it was much harder to sing with the bass, much different than singing with guitar.

MIKE GORDON: Mm-hmm. Yeah.

LINDA: So when you began singing, did you pay attention to that? Had that issue come up for you?

MIKE GORDON: I first started singing a lot in my high school band. For a few years before then, I was taking guitar lessons, singing along, making cassette tapes around the house, and so, um, there was already a lot of singing being done at that point, with doing a lot of Phish . . . bass players often talk about that—with guitar you can strum and your hand keeps going. If you're playing lead, you can sort of stop playing, sing a line, and start to fill in (*plays air guitar*). So both of those make it easy to sing, but with bass, it *has* to keep going, and when it's syncopated, it's very hard to have syncopated bass parts along with singing syncopated, and many bass players talk about that—one of them has to go on autopilot to some degree. You can really be easily improvising on both, letting loose on both. That always became difficult, and there are—even now—some things in my own repertoire that I can hardly ever get. Like a moment, it's always when they're both syncopated and they're off from each other, and the voice follows a sixteenth note before the bass and then after, so that just makes it more difficult. It's probably with the piano that I first started singing, and then with the guitar.

LINDA: What kind of music did you sing with the piano?

MIKE GORDON: Before the high school band I was just picking out songs from the radio. Actually I have these cassettes I've gone through, and they're all archived on Dropbox now, everything I've ever recorded, so I'm just thinking back now. 'Cause on those cassettes I recorded, I'll hear mostly songs from the radio that I taped, and then I'll hear myself making something up or doing a mock-up. It's seldom that I would find a tape of me singing straight heartfelt singing, apart from one song I wrote for my girlfriend in high school. But more typically (*laughs*)—um, I have these tapes the members of Phish love to hear.

My mom, who always listened to singers with various ethnic accents, liked these crooner types. So, one time when my parents were out, I wanted to make fun of that. So I got my brother to play castanets and an organ I'd rented, and we made up a song called "Savacksa Groovyarey," and we'd do it over and over again and most of the time I'm yelling at my brother, which everyone likes to hear (*laughs*). So I guess until then, probably about a tween, I was still just singing silly things. There are a couple of tapes of me singing Beatles or Jim Croce. We used to go up to the Ninety-Nine Restaurant and listen to the guitarist there singing songs like that. And I was in music camp, was in a choir—just coincidently, we did *The Wiz*.

LINDA: You told me once that you remember lying on the sofa with the bass on top of you just playing the strings and feeling the vibrations.

MIKE GORDON: Yeah, and the guitar.

LINDA: Can you remember a time when you felt something like that about singing?

MIKE GORDON: Right, my gut-feeling reaction is that, honestly, I think that—let me answer that in more than one way. I think that my relationship to playing got deeper first. For me, singing was just something that people did because there were lyrics, rather than because it's an emotional experience. One thing I remember, and Sue has the same memory for her, is learning all the verses to "American Pie" when I first started playing guitar, and going in the living room and saying, "I want you all to listen to me sing all the verses," and then I was pissed that they were singing along a bit. So that was the first moment when I was getting into singing. Then the song for my first girlfriend, and the funny songs I made up for a laugh, some of those were getting kind of emotional. I think I had more breakthrough moments later. Then Trey and I and the whole band started taking singing lessons. First, we had this woman who made us hold these long notes and tried to get us into the meditation of it, letting them travel over the hills. So that kind of awakened my idea, my appreciation, that the voice is so central, and in the middle of us, and such a pure feeling when it's allowed to resonate freely. And then we had this other woman, a local jazz singer—we still make fun of some of her catchphrases—but she wanted us to improvise with our voices, because that's what we were doing with instruments. And that's where the vocal jam for "You Enjoy Myself" came from—which is, you know, just ten minutes of making weird noises and melodies up on the scratch and trash usually to end the set.

But getting to be able to say that I'm getting into this emotionally and feeling it, there were just some moments. . . . I remember my girlfriend saying, "Do you even like singing or do you just do it?" By then, I had already had some of these experiences when I didn't just do it. But just that fact that she said that meant a lot, and I became aware that there was a difference between getting into it and just phoning it in.

LINDA: Interesting. But at the same time, you told me once that you can't imagine music without singing?

MIKE GORDON: Well, I can imagine it, if it's a jazz band or orchestra. Then I can appreciate it, but I just want to have a band that's vocal. I mean, it would be pretty backwards for me to say, I can't imagine it because some of the peak experiences of my life are these jams that are twenty minutes and about twelve minutes in, it really gels, and we're taking flight, and all that—and usually, those don't include singing. It's just my desire to have singing in the band. And we've had over the years, we've had band members that have brought instrumental tunes, and for me, it works to an extent, but it's really rare that I feel comfortable putting in instrumental tunes because we have jams anyway, so I'm not looking to put them into the set.

LINDA: What's that about?

MIKE GORDON: You mean why?

LINDA: Yeah, I mean, you're a bass player, and you jam.

MIKE GORDON: Yeah, for me, the twenty minutes jamming doesn't even really have significance unless you set it up with a song, and ideally come back with a song. When I was five years old and *Abbey Road* came out, we listened to it for a decade. Those songs were strumming my heartstrings. Even though I may not have been always singing along, I was connecting with other emotions and crushes. So nothing is really deeper than that for me. So if it's going to be a long jam, for me, it can't just start and end on a tone. For me, it's not going to be as interesting if there isn't some song. In the jam band world, which is a horrible phrase, it doesn't necessarily matter if the sound of the jam is connected to the emotion of the lyric, but inevitably it's going to be related somehow or other.

As I get older, I'm even more interested in writing and singing songs, and less interested in jamming, although the jamming can still be a peak experience. I guess in terms of what touches me, what touches my heart, is probably someone singing, at the apex of being a performing musician. When I was the bass player in Dead & Company . . . No, it was earlier, when we did that "Move Me, Break Me" for Jerry's seventieth birthday, Bob Weir got all of us together in this room with twenty people—and I really appreciate his singing a lot, especially the way that he honors the moment and the emotion of the song more than anything. He said to us in the little catering room before the gig, no matter what any of you are playing, the singing is the *face* of the song, and nothing else matters, nothing else should be in your consciousness. And for him, even after 3,500 Grateful Dead shows for millions of people with tons of jamming, the song is still the crux. And, you know, he's someone who's listened to a lot of American traditional music from Robert Johnson to country and bluegrass. So, he's been a big influence on me, and he's embraced and perpetuated the fact that American culture is being carried on through song.

LINDA: Yes!

MIKE GORDON: As was the Hebrew culture in my Hebrew day school. So for me, it's not going to have that significance without that tradition in there.

LINDA: Yeah, and it's actually the same with American art song—it's a catalog of American history and culture. But I want to say that I remember that concert you're talking about. We'd been working together for about three months. There was a time difference, so I actually fell asleep for some of it, but I heard you sang "He's Gone" that we had worked on. The concert was streaming, and there was a chat box with fans commenting while you were singing. The fans were just going wild talking about how beautiful your singing was, and I remember Bob Weir was watching you during this really beautiful chorus with a sort of shocked look. Suddenly, he just leaned in to the mic and did a soft growl. It was just the perfect emotional mix to add to your singing.

MIKE GORDON: Yeah, and I remember listening to that song on the radio the day Jerry died and the DJ saying, this is why we're playing that song.

LINDA: That was certainly coming through when you sang that night. I'm not surprised by what you said about Bob because it comes across when he sings that the lyrics and song are really guiding him, I sense that when he sings.

MIKE GORDON: In his voice, yeah.

LINDA: When you spoke at Berklee last week, you talked about performing and this feeling of peak experience that is sort of transformational, like dreaming while you're awake. I'm wondering how singing fits into that. I know it happens when you're jamming, but when does it happen when you're singing? Does it relate to that "He's Gone" experience?

MIKE GORDON: There are times when it's all dialed in, and even though the bass is playing, that stuff is on automatic, all the music is on automatic (*plays air guitar again*), maybe Scott and I are hitting a harmony, just right on, and I have this feeling of my brain squeezing in a good way (*laughs*). Like, let's say you were in, like in the summer in 110 degrees, and you just suddenly got a cool towel, that kind of, like a catharsis, suddenly it's like—*whoosh*—like it's just happening and it's coming through us, just like in an incredible peak experience jam just happens, and the music is playing itself. Those lyrics feel like they're coming from God, straight through our mouths and out into the room.

LINDA: Can you think of any specific songs when that may have happened recently?

MIKE: Well, the first one that comes to mind, I can remember one time in the studio, singing "Steps." I had actually been having a hard time with it, and then after working with you on Skype for a while, went back to it, and maybe having only three hours sleep affected me—and I got to the high part, about going away, and I just started crying every time. Something just flicked in my emotional being, and every time I started singing it, it was just emotional. But it wasn't a bad emotion, it was like this needed to come out, flow out, drain, and this song and the fact that I get to sing it provides the release. And so there's an example of feeling so thankful that I get to do this, and that's something that wasn't just going to come through bass playing, it needed to be sung. It's lyrics, and it's voice, and really, maybe even more, melody and tone and vowels than the actual lyrics themselves that create this emotion.

REFLECTIONS

There are three aspects of singing that Mike Gordon mentions that we've already talked about in this book; songs as part of culture and tradition, songs as emotional bonding, and the transformational power of performing. What examples do you have in your life—as a singer, performer, or just in your daily life—that demonstrate these three aspects of singing?

- Culture and tradition

- Emotional bonding

- Transformations

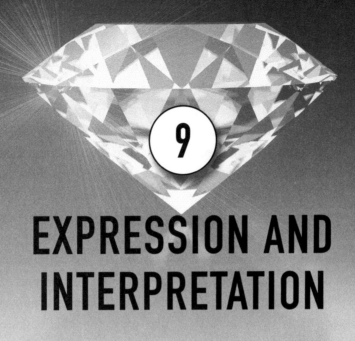

9

EXPRESSION AND INTERPRETATION

Amidst the shadowed darkness, she cautiously steps between heavy velvet curtains,
finally arriving at the pitch-black corner of stage right. Violins, violas, and cellos
buzz and hum. Like pre-concert partygoers, they're mingling with softly chattering
flutes, clarinets, and oboes. Their quiet cacophony rises and falls as the orchestra
slowly settles. The house lights darken, and she steps into the light, first drifting,
then submerging into another world; where everyday experiences like sleeping and
eating become meaningless; where sensations of sound, touch and light become
extraordinary; where there is only music, words, and message.

—LB

I didn't know it at the time, but I began my journey to become a vocologist in the year 2000 in Vienna, Austria. I had just joined the voice faculty of the Vienna Conservatory in the musical theater department. One crisp fall morning, as I walked across a bridge over the Danube Canal, I suddenly realized I was very excited! I couldn't wait to arrive at the conservatory. Feeling like I was getting ready to go onstage, I realized that teaching was as much fun as performing. Like many new teachers, I was discovering how exciting it is to teach people to sing beautifully and enjoy their singing.

And I had a dream. My dream was that each and every one of my students would learn to sing in an easy, comfortable, expressive manner without developing muscle tension or analytical thinking patterns, without shutting down their instincts and intuition, without getting lost in a muddle of jargon and theoretical analysis, and without losing their connection to why they began singing in the first place.

I had spent hours in late-night conversations with fellow singers who were struggling with consistency and reliability in their voices, debating various voice teachers and methods, wondering if their high notes were going to be "on" at the next audition. And although I had studied with several teachers in the United States and Europe, putting together bits and pieces to develop a voice that I could use "on the road," it had been a frustrating experience. I knew and worked with many singers who had had the same frustrations.

I envisioned a world where singers would always be excited instead of frustrated, equipped with *real* tools to work with their voices, no matter what conditions they faced.

I was determined, just like you are now. You're doing the work to discover how to use your voice, staying focused so you can sing freely, expressively, and powerfully, no matter what you sing. You've been practicing exercises to train coordination, improve tone, and manage dynamics. You've learned many tools you can use to face the challenges of performing, auditioning, and recording. And you have strategies to keep yourself moving forward in all aspects of your singing life.

It's time to take a closer look at singing the music you love and develop your ability to share your message and the message in the music and words.

9.1 EXERCISE
Song Interpretation

1. Choose a song. This can be any style of song.

2. Print out or write out the lyrics of the song.

3. Read through the lyrics or text and write *one* sentence that summarizes the message. Be specific. Is the song about someone who is frustrated, sad, hopeful, excited? Is the singer speaking to themselves, to a lover, or to the universe? What is the *transformation* during the song? (I could write a chapter on this topic but we're almost at the end of this book.)

Each song or aria has its own story, more specific than the story of the opera or musical it may be part of, and very specific to the emotional life of the person in the text/lyric.

"Happy Birthday to you,
Happy Birthday to you,
Happy Birthday, dear Reader,
Happy Birthday to you."¹

The message of this song is "I/we wish you happiness". The song begins, nicely, sweetly, with a simple rhythm matching every syllable to a beat (except the message-word of "happy"—that gets two syllables on one note, making the word sound happy). But, then the song gets more serious, more dramatic. With the word "dear" we know this song is speaking to someone who is important. We only say "dear" to people we love. Then a specific person's name appears and it gets four beats, an entire measure! The name of the person gets the most significant rhythmic attention. Finally, just in case you weren't paying attention, the longer rhythm is repeated on "to you," so the value of the person is highlighted again. As an added bonus, if a group of people sing this together, invariably some of the singers improvise harmony on the words " to you," so it sounds louder and *more* triumphant. If you want to make sure you have optimum resonance on this song, make sure you sing "Birthday" on the third line, when the pitch changes, with rounded lips, like a small pout, so the pronunciation will be clear and the frequencies and harmonics with align nicely. That's much better than reaching up for the note and singing "Bahthday" out of tune or in a "yell" quality. Even with a simple song like this, there is a transformation from "I'm happy" to " I love this person so much and I want to show them they are important." If anyone has any doubt about the value of singing to humans, they need only sing this song; using voices, usually in a group, to celebrate a member of the tribe, making sure they understand how much they are valued, even improvising to create more volume and energy.

> "When humans want to say something very important that has a high emotional value, we do so with our singing voice."
> —Renée Fleming

4. Now, go back to the song you have chosen. Can you go through your song the same way I've done with "Happy Birthday"? Here are a few hints:

The main message of almost all songs and arias:

"I wish . . ."
"I should have . . ."
"I want . . ."
"Remember when . . ."

Most of the time, songs are about love:
celebrating love
declaring love
expressing the pain of lost love or unrequited love.

Pay attention to sudden changes in harmony pitch and rhythm. Many times, the changes occur in the music just before the melody makes the changes, but sometimes the melody leads the way. The changes are a signal that the emotional life of the singer is changing, too.

5. Visualize and tactilize for each of the important words. This may be as simple as a color or as complex as an entire scene playing out in your mind's eye. Be specific: Is the sky blue or grey? Is she wearing a red dress or a blue dress? Is it a windy day or hot and humid? Is the love interest in the room, or walking away?

6. Play the music, either on an instrument, a recording, or even in your imagination, and say the words while the music is playing. Can you feel and hear where the words fall in the music and rhythm? You are now connecting to the groove, or feel, of the music in relation to the words. In an art song or opera aria, there's also a rhythmic feel connected to the text. Can you feel how the composer has connected the text to the movement of the music?

You can do this exercise with several different types of songs to develop your awareness of how song lyrics and texts communicate the message of the music. You can also try this exercise with a song you've sung many times before. You'll find you may have a new way of experiencing a song you've been singing for a long time.

9.2 EXERCISE

Actualize

How many words can you find to describe the message of a song? Can you fill in the circles and make meaningful connections? Write words within the circles and make connections when you can. Write as fast as you can, without stopping to think about it. Are there any words that should go outside the circles?

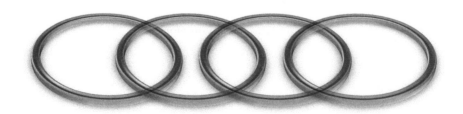

Why do we sing? Survival instincts may be the source for a human's complex singing ability, but now singing is an art form. How did we get here?

Recent fMRIs provide a visual for things we've instinctively known for thousands of years: singing and music evoke emotional responses that are the same as those we experience in everyday life. In fact, fMRIs show that neural activity during singing and listening to music take place in every region of the brain, and it may be the brain's most complex activity. Now that we can see the all-encompassing neural activity of singing, we get a better sense of why singing shifted from survival needs to the vast music industry we have today. It's part of our cultural evolution, perhaps even our *neural* evolution. We've turned singing into an art form, just as food preparation, a basic need, has created the art of cooking, and our basic need for shelter has created architecture. Considering the evolution of human culture over the last several thousand years, it seems that we continue developing our music and singing abilities because we seek greater and greater emotional intensity and more and more varied emotional experiences.

In Conversation with Mina Alali and Arlene Mordeno

You've been doing a great deal of study and work throughout this training, but I'm sure you're thinking about what could be next once you are able to express what you want with your voice. The singers I coach are at different stages of their careers, but some wonder how to get started.

Read ahead to see what I found out when I sat down with the up-and-coming pop singer Mina Alali and her manager, Arlene Mordeno, from Kick-a-Beat Records.

LINDA: Arlene, I've been really impressed watching the trajectory of the work you're doing with Mina's career so I'm really glad to have a chance to chat with you about it. I was curious about how Mina could get such a great start to her performing career—then I read that you have a business background?

ARLENE: Yes, I'm currently working in information technology.

LINDA: I think your business background and your music background as an accomplished child pianist make you a great person to work with a young artist. Do you think that's what's helped you work with Mina?

ARLENE: Yes, it's just like another business, there's always a product, and in this case, it's the talent—it could be a song, or a brand. In this case, the brand is Mina. Also, I was in a program under Imelda Marcos in the Philippines as a pianist—the competition was fierce—I realized you needed to hustle, you need to do everything in your power to be successful, and you need somebody to back you up, a force or a group of people to support you and tell you what's going to work. You can make bad choices or collaborate with bad people and end up with nothing or a bad reputation.

LINDA: Yes! The classical music world has the same traps.

ARLENE: So I knew how it was out there being a young person trying to make it—I don't know everything—all I can do is try my best to support Mina and make sure she's put out in a good light and doesn't collaborate with the wrong people—making sure her brand is consistent and doesn't get washed out.

LINDA: Now it makes sense to me, since you were in a high-pressure music industry as a child. One of the things I especially love about what you're doing with Mina is the stepwise progression—how she's been allowed to really grow into things in an organic way, rather than being pushed out to make money fast and do things that are beyond her or not authentic to her.

ARLENE: Yes, I'm not a big label who needs to "make money on you now or I'll cut you off and replace you with another artist"—it's very organic because we want to be true to ourselves. There are still some moves that I regret—I think about some steps and I think, *Maybe we shouldn't have done that so soon*—or *Maybe I should have collaborated more with her in writing that song so she knows it from her heart because she cowrote it.* We've got a contract for two years, but she's got a lot of freedom to move around social media and post her own videos. I remind her to stay consistent with her brand. I'm not out there to rush and make money off her. I'm glad you noticed that!

LINDA: Yes, it's so important for her vocal and her artistic development, both of those things. Could you tell me about the video production for "22 Cents Less," the song about women earning twenty-two cents less per dollar than men? Such a great video!

ARLENE: Yes! That was done in Boston. Mina actually gave me the title for that song—and I recognized it immediately because I've experienced this issue in the corporate world. So when she gave me that title, I said "Oh really, you're willing to take that risk with this title? I'm game, let's do it." So we wrote the song, and then, since Mina was at Berklee, I decided to fly over to Boston. I hired a production company—and what was nice about that video is *a lot* of women volunteered to do it. I saw the casting call in

Backstage.com and it said it was an unpaid job—but *a lot* of women volunteered to do it.

LINDA: Wow!

ARLENE: Because of the cause, you know. The first idea was to show shoes—so showing a lot of different kind of shoes—like grungy boots walking on the street, then a pair of high heels—representing women going to work every day in all kinds of work. The subject is a little dark, but the message of the song is encouraging, that things are not going to be that way forever—things are going to change.

LINDA: The women crying in the video are really authentic—I know their reaction is real because I've shown the video to many women and men who have cried also. When Mina first showed me the demo track for the song—she had it on her phone in a lesson so we could work on the vocals, I was really moved. So I found the song really compelling but also really fun.

ARLENE: Yes, it's funny, today's generation who haven't lived the message yet—they dance to it and have a lot of fun without realizing the message. The other thing that was cool about that song, is it came up on the jumbo billboard in Times Square for a few days.

LINDA: Yes, I saw that. Did you arrange that or did it just happen?

ARLENE: It happened because I contracted PR Newswire to do a national splash of the song. They have a permanent billboard there in Times Square. They really liked the cover art of the album, the photo of Mina with her head to the side, with just the song title "22 Cents Less"—that was intriguing to them. I was really surprised that they picked that to be in the Jumbotron—I don't want to be a reverse sexist, but usually the large press houses are run by males and they may have been offended by that message. Not everybody supports that message. So I was really surprised because I had really hired them to do press releases.

LINDA: That's fantastic how that worked out. How did you find and choose to work with Mina?

ARLENE: I was taking voice lesson in Canada so I could get better at making demos of my songs because I'm a songwriter and publisher—I had sold a few songs overseas, but I haven't had a hit in the US. So I met her in the studio and made the demo. I hired her as a studio singer—and little by little I heard about what she wanted to do. I had spent years dealing with rejection as a songwriter. I had belonged to songwriters' associations where we'd pitch our songs to industry professionals and they'd hear the songs for twenty seconds and reject them outright. So then I got it: the music industry is all about networking and about who you know. You have to make it happen for yourself instead of waiting for someone to pick you up and make it happen for you. That's why I said to Mina, "Why don't we partner up? I'm going to do this and let's see what happens."

LINDA: Fabulous—that is so true—just about everybody has had to deal with a lot of rejection and there are just those few moments that propel us forward and make things start to happen. It is amazing how much creative work requires you to hustle as well!

Mina, one of the things I noticed about you is that you took a great deal of initiative before you even met Arlene or came to Berklee—you created an a cappella group, gigging and recording on your own. What do you think inspired you to take action with your music?

MINA: I think it was as simple as wanting to share my message with others—I know I was twelve years old when I starting working on the computer with production in GarageBand (music recording software)—I knew that no one else was doing that, so I wanted my unique thing—and it was so organically discovered—I loved to sing, and I just kept looking to do as much as I could.

LINDA: I remember when I was a child and the first time I heard opera on PBS—I had already been singing and studying music for a long time, but I just knew as soon as I saw that opera on PBS—that was what I wanted for the rest of my life. Even though I was about twelve years old. I was wondering if you had a similar experience?

MINA: Yes, I remember I saw one of my best friends do *Oliver* at school. It was her first show, and I thought she was amazing, and I just thought, *I want to learn how to do that*—but I wanted to do it my own way. I was pretty competitive, but in a good way. I wanted to be my best.

LINDA: Did you get that from your family?

MINA: Absolutely—my dad is a strong believer in doing your best, being the best at whatever you can do. It bled into everything I was doing.

LINDA: Cool! About what time did you start thinking about working with a coach or voice teacher?

MINA: I started pretty young with a classical teacher—I didn't know the difference in genres—there was so much talk about breathing and stuff and the songs were not pop—they were certainly not inspiring—so I didn't want to continue. But in my senior year of high school, my mom and I took a tour of Berklee, and I knew this was the only school I wanted to go to. I applied and decided I needed to work with a coach to prepare for the audition.

LINDA: And when you came to Berklee, you got placed in my studio—I think it was kind of a shock to your system (*laughs*).

MINA: No, I mean, yes, in a way, but it was a good shock.

LINDA: I felt like you had accepted some kind of limitations with your voice—certain notes, or range—and you felt that was basically your voice. Is that true?

MINA: Yes, I think I did, the thing that shocked me the most is—I just thought my head voice was just weak. I wished I could sound the same up there as when I belted down here, and then you introduced me to the mixed voice, which was, like, an entirely new part of my voice that I hadn't discovered yet. But I think I had unconsciously decided that I wouldn't be able to do it and had just been working around it. I thought some people were born able to do that, and I just wasn't one of them—so, yes, it can be learned. And also, singing shouldn't feel hard, it should never feel hard. You don't have to strain. That was huge for me. I would think I needed to reach up to get everything.

LINDA: And now that you're performing, you can see the benefit because you have time and space in your body and mind to pay attention to music, lyrics, and all the other things that you needed to perform.

MINA: Absolutely. And it only makes sense now because I see these huge artists doing two to three month tours, and if I stuck with that mind-set—was still reaching—I'd never be able to do it. So you have to develop that healthy voice in order to survive as a singer.

LINDA: Definitely. I saw somewhere that you said, "I always find that I'm more productive and happier when I'm working on something slightly outside my comfort zone." Certainly, working on the mix was outside your comfort zone at first, as it is for many singers, but many people are afraid of working outside their comfort zones. What do you think makes you happier?

MINA: I think, growing up in a small suburb, by the time I reached high school, I felt like I had done and seen everything, so I really wanted to get out of there and do something new. So I decided to study abroad in France. I struggled a lot in the first few months—not because of homesickness or anything but because I had to learn the language and deal with a lot of unknowns. But I had never been happier because I was using a new part of my brain.

LINDA: And that gives you energy.

MINA: Exactly. And you're focusing on bigger and better things. That became, like, my fuel—just having a project to always be working on. I'd hate to not be productive because there's always stuff to be doing.

REFLECTIONS

Arlene and Mina are both highly motivated, creative artists. Their creative work is very important to them but they're also both driven to share their message with as many people as possible, hustling to do the work that will keep them moving forward while they continue to focus on perfecting their craft.

Mina said she sees how more experienced singers work hard when they're on tour, singing all the time, traveling, sleeping in a different place every night, and it made her realize that it's a highly stressful and physically demanding job! Singing at home or in a recording studio for a few days is much less demanding on the voice, body, and mind than going on tour.

o Have you already noticed this when you have had a long rehearsal schedule or other demands on your time?

o Which tools and strategies in this book can you use to manage vocal fatigue?

o If you've already been touring, do you recall which strategies helped you?

o Which behaviors were harmful?

10

EXPAND FLEXIBILITY

*I'm singing what I want to sing based on the emotion of what that day feels like.
That's what comes out of my mouth and guitar. That impacts people.
They know anything can happen.*

—John Mayer, American singer-songwriter, guitarist, and producer

Flexibility in singing is required in every genre. In classical music, there can be many small rhythmic patterns and long melodic lines on only one vowel, as in coloratura. In R&B, it's common to sing several notes on one word or part of a word to express the mood of the singer; jazz requires an ability to move easily and quickly, even if you don't scat; and rock singers sing licks, small melodic lines at the end of words and phrases for expression. No matter what genre of music you sing, your voice needs to be able to move easily with a relaxed larynx.

That's why the previous chapters were focused on developing your mix and your

ability to maintain a relaxed larynx and consistent contact throughout your range. You need that freedom *before* you can work on flexibility. If you sing riffs and coloratura without having a relaxed larynx, you may have trouble managing dynamics and pitch. You may begin tightening your throat to control the notes, which will make you feel tired and limit your resonance. So, during the following training, be sure to check in on your voice using the tools from previous chapters whenever anything seems like it's not quite right, like intonation, vibrato, rising larynx, or unclear vowels.

The larynx and its posture, or position, are a hot topic among voice professionals.

Today many different opinions about larynx position have developed from trends in singing aesthetic. Beginning with the musical *Annie* on Broadway in 1976, and with the rise of the singer/songwriter, heavy metal and other cultural trends, singers have developed a wide variety of sounds that challenge age-old concepts. Humans are capable of producing a wide range of sounds with their voices, but singing for a profession, or even as a serious hobby, can place a heavy burden on the two tiny ligaments in your larynx.

You can get a better understanding of the best way to sing comfortably and with least amount of effort in your throat by considering how the larynx works in daily life. Its main job is to prevent foreign objects from entering the lungs. When food and drink go down the tube leading to the stomach (the esophagus) there's a little cover (the epiglottis) that closes over the larynx to prevent anything from getting into your lungs (the trachea). At the same time, your larynx goes up, creating more room in the esophagus and helping the food or drink move downward. There is a set of muscles in your neck that make it possible for the larynx to go up for swallowing (the digastrics). We can't voluntarily hold the larynx up.

The only circumstances in which the larynx goes up and *stays* up are found in choking and drowning. When water goes down your trachea suddenly, your body has two defenses. The first is to cough: your larynx and vocal folds work hard to

get that stuff *out* as fast as possible, so your vocal folds slam shut and your larynx goes up. The second is a laryngeal spasm. This is an involuntary movement that closes off the trachea quickly to prevent water from getting into your lungs.

I had a real-world experience that taught me a lot about the larynx and the benefits of training. In my first scuba dive after getting certified, I went on an easy river dive: not deep, and close to the boat and two shorelines. After I geared up and I'd done all the proper checks, the boat captain decided he wanted to be "helpful." Just before I entered the water, he checked the valve on my tank while I was wearing it and turned it almost all the way off. I didn't even know he had touched it. After about ten minutes underwater trying to figure out why I was struggling for air, I decided to return to the surface. As I ascended, my air supply was completely gone; the underwater pressure had fully closed the valve. I was so relieved to get to the surface where I quickly pulled the regulator out of my mouth. But no air came in! I was above water with my mouth open, trying to inhale, but getting no air! I couldn't get any air in my flotation device either. I was wearing about thirty pounds of equipment, so I knew I would go under very quickly if something didn't change. Suddenly, my scuba diving coach "appeared" and shouted at me, "Focus!" I could actually "see" my coach in the water nearby. I gave the boat captain a distress signal. He jumped in and began swimming toward me. I leaned back to float on the surface, extended my arms while kicking my feet to stay afloat. I felt my larynx "choking" me. I didn't understand why I couldn't breath, I was in a sort of shocked denial, but my scuba instructor was still "shouting" at me. Suddenly, I focused like a laser. Without consciously thinking about it, I dropped my diaphragm and my larynx, and air came flooding in to my lungs.

I didn't know at the time, but I had had a nonfatal drowning because water had entered my lungs. When that happens, your body's defense mechanism closes off your airway to prevent more water from entering. This is called a laryngeal spasm, which keeps your larynx high, in the swallowing position with your vocal folds slammed shut. Unfortunately, this also prevents air from getting in. In drowning, laryngeal spasm leads to a lack of oxygen, which leads to loss of consciousness, followed very quickly by sinking and drowning. I survived because my motor performance is highly trained. I had been trained to *focus* by my scuba coach, and I had automatic function of my diaphragm and larynx from voice training. I didn't consciously choose to drop my diaphragm or my larynx; it just happened automatically when I focused because the neural pathways

> The larynx does *slightly* rise or adjust its position when we're singing in different ranges to accommodate the stretch and relaxation of the vocal folds, but it's a very tiny movement. We can't really see or feel it except a sensation of the change in vibration.

for that motor movement are very firmly established.

These are two real-life situations when the larynx goes up and stays there. If your singing and feeling like something is tight, closing your throat, most likely that's because your larynx is too high.

From acoustic studies, using a spectrograph, we also know that singing with a higher larynx changes the sound quality (e.g., screaming, like in fear, is done with a higher larynx position). In the musical *Wicked* the sensational Idina Menzel solidified her celebrity status by using this high larynx scream for her character. She was playing a hysterical witch, so screaming was appropriate for the role. She maintains her approach to singing with high doses of rest and rehabilitation. She's an experienced performer and a consummate artist but the burden of maintaining high larynx singing is heavy. Like a horror movie that makes you jump in your chair, high larynx singing can cause an instinctive response from listeners.

> Screaming in some kinds of rock, heavy metal, or punk rock is different. Techniques with glottal fry and managing the microphone allow you to make special effects that won't tire your voice or put your larynx in an uncomfortable position.

Singers who sing with a high larynx pay a price for it in the long run. It's not fun to feel tired in your throat all the time, having to go to a teacher to rehabilitate your voice after a big tour, never knowing if you're going to be too tired to perform at your best. You'll enjoy your singing and career much more if it doesn't cost you so much of your vocal freedom. Besides, given the choice, in my experience, most people don't want to hear people yelling onstage or at auditions. The most common complaint I hear from casting directors is that they get tired and stressed listening to auditions because so many singers are yelling at them.

And, consider how your body is informed from a behavior that normally only occurs in an emergency situation.

Remember that you can always sing with extended tongue if you're feeling uncomfortable. Go back to a previous scale series whenever you need to relax, focus, or balance your singing.

Remember, your brain not only sends signals to your body, it also receives them. That's why the goal is a relaxed, low larynx. Not pushed down or pulled up, just relaxed and stable. In this position, the larynx is free to do whatever it needs to do to make pitches throughout your range and in all dynamic levels. You can achieve this when you tactilize, audicize and visualize, "rum-tum-tum"—and make the dopey dog your new best friend.

◆ ◆ ◆

Before singing the scales for flexibility, prepare your voice, mind, and body. Begin singing with a scale series that feels easy and that you enjoy. Begin with SOVTs, then try lip rolls or tongue rolls.

10.1 SCALE SERIES
The Broken Octave

Sing the broken octave on lip rolls

1. Choose the scale.

2. Play or listen before you begin singing.

3. Say "could." Audicize the vowel. Keep relaxed, chubby lips.

4. This scale may feel lighter than some of the previous scales. Take time to sense the fluidity and buoyancy of singing in motion.

Sing one octave lower than written

Can you sing evenly and smoothly without your larynx rising?

Chart Your Experience

Answer yes, no, don't know.

AFTER SINGING   **AFTER RECORDING**

_____   Couldn't control it.   _____

_____   Felt tight in my throat.   _____

_____   Vowel changed in the upper notes.   _____

_____   Sound got quieter on the lower notes.   _____

_____   Couldn't feel the beat.   _____

_____   Sang louder as the scale went higher.   _____

_____   The scale felt easy.   _____

_____   Couldn't hear the upper pitches.   _____

_____   Volume throughout the scale was even.   _____

_____   Breathing felt easy and calm without gasping.   _____

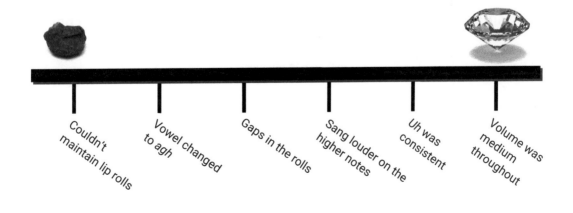

Can you write down what you tactilized, audicized, and visualized while you were singing? What aspects felt positive when you sang the scale? What aspects felt like they could be improved?

_____

_____

_____

COACHING TIP

Visualize the scale as a straight line rather than a line going up and down.
Record yourself. Ask a buddy to watch or listen. Chart your experiences again.

10.1A
Broken octave on oo as in google

Now sing the broken octave on *oo*. This may feel very "hooty" or light. You won't feel the same contact you may have experienced in previous scales, but you should still feel an evenness—so no sudden changes in feeling or volume during the scale. Maintain the hooty voice. Can you increase the tempo?

Chart Your Experience

Answer yes, no, or don't know.

AFTER SINGING		AFTER RECORDING
_____	Felt tight in my throat.	_____
_____	Couldn't maintain even volume.	_____
_____	Vowel changed in the upper notes.	_____
_____	Sound got quieter on the lower notes.	_____

_____   Couldn't feel the beat.   _____

_____   Sang louder on the upper pitches.   _____

_____   Scale felt easy and free.   _____

_____   Breathing felt easy and calm without gasping.   _____

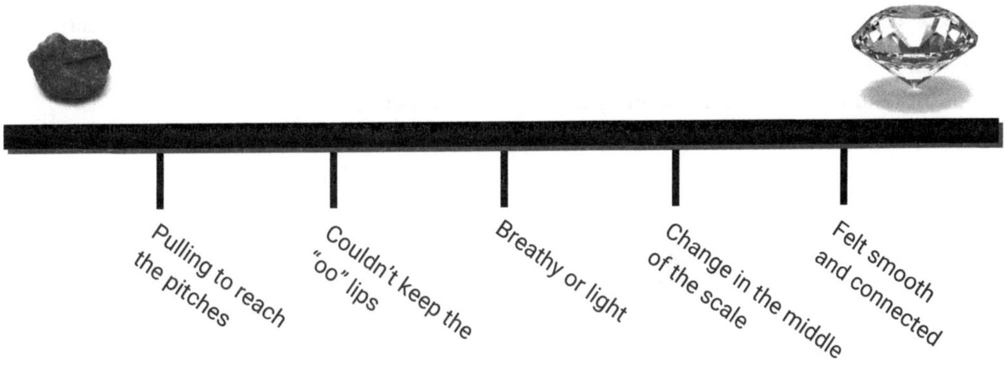

Pulling to reach the pitches

Couldn't keep the "oo" lips

Breathy or light

Change in the middle of the scale

Felt smooth and connected

COACHING TIP

Audicize the hooty voice. Keep the volume even. Sink into the first tone of each scale.

Can you write what you tactilized, audicized, and visualized while you were singing? What aspects felt good when you sang the scale? What aspects felt like they could be improved?

_____

_____

_____

DEBRIEF

Can you write your own debrief? What happened? Could you connect the tone in the lower and upper parts of the scale?

_____

_____

_____

Inhale _____

Effort _____

Resonance _____

COACHING TIP

If you're not sure you can sing the vowel throughout the scale, go back to doing the scale on lip rolls or tongue rolls. Can you visualize and audicize the *oo* vowel while you're singing on the rolls or trills?

Record and invite a buddy. Chart your experiences again.

10.2 SCALE SERIES
More Vibrato

You can continue developing your ability to sing with vibrato by audicizing when you sing. Continue shaking your hand while you sing each note, keeping it loose, relaxed, and fluid. Can you tactilize the vibration when you're singing with vibrato?

1. Choose the scale for your voice.

2. Audicize the *oo* vowel. Tactilize buoyancy: airy but not breathy!

3. Sing each note with vibrato—the flow should be easy, like a gentle stream, not like a crashing river!

4. Connect the notes—you may feel the air and vibration moving while you're singing but you don't feel anything "shifting" or moving in your throat. You can point your index finger under your chin to find out if you're moving the back of your tongue or anything else.

Female

maintain "whistle" lips   *keep moving your hand while you sing*   *even consistent volume*

you can continue higher if you feel comfortable.

continue singing back down the scale

Male One
Sing one octave lower than written

maintain "whistle" lips   *keep moving your hand while you sing*   *even consistent volume*

you can continue higher if you feel comfortable.

continue singing back down the scale

Male Two

maintain "whistle" lips   *keep moving your hand while you sing*   *even conssitent volume*

continue singing back down the scale

Take your time with each tone. Can you gently wiggle your jaw a little bit from side to side while singing? Is your stomach relaxed when you inhale? You may feel like space is opening behind your face, or there is an "airy" feeling in your head.

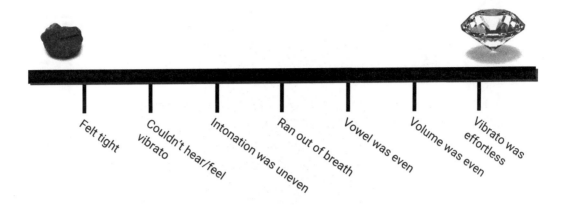

Begin the first tone of each scale with the right touch. Do you feel buoyant?

Can you write what you tactilized, audicized, and visualized while you were singing? What aspects felt positive when you sang the scale? What aspects felt like they could be improved?

_____

_____

_____

DEBRIEF

If you feel something moving when you're changing notes, sing the exercise on *mm* with your tongue between your lips. Reduce the volume until you feel you can sing it without anything moving. Slowly increase the volume until you can sing in your "talking" volume without feeling movement or "shifting" in your throat. It may take time to develop this ability.

COACHING TIP

When you feel like this exercise is easy, and the vibrato is consistent and controlled, you can try doing the exercises faster, and on different vowels, like *ee*, *oh*, and *uh*.

Record yourself. Write some notes about what you sensed again.

Remember to maintain the shape and sound of each vowel during every scale. You may adjust the mouth opening as you change range, but your lips stay in the vowel shape.

10.3 SCALE SERIES
Staccato

Singing staccato means each note is very short but very clear and clean. At the same time, your mouth and throat feel loose and open. Can you develop the skill to make contact in just your voice, with a clear, even vowel and equal volume throughout the scale? Sing this exercise first on *oo* as in *google*, then later try *ee* as in *eat* and *uh* as in *rum-tum-tum*.

- Choose the scale for your voice type.
- Shake out your body and hands before you begin.
- Point your index finger under your chin while you singing. The soft part under your chin should stay soft while your singing, and it should remain still.

Feel the muscles in your body drop or release at the end of each scale. The air comes in automatically. Keep your lips in the form of the vowel *oo* like whistling. Avoid singing with an H sound at the beginning of each note. Tactilize a nice, easy touch for the start of each scale.

DEBRIEF

What did you notice about your sound in this scale? What did you notice about the feel of this scale? Tight? Clear? Smooth? Light? Buoyant? Write your sensations.

_____

_____

_____

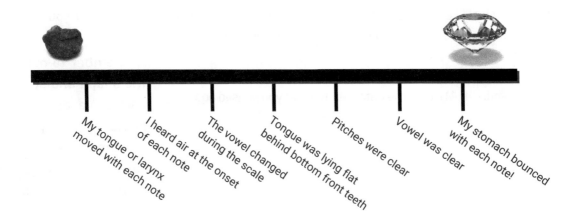

My tongue or larynx moved with each note

I heard air at the onset of each note

The vowel changed during the scale

Tongue was lying flat behind bottom front teeth

Pitches were clear

Vowel was clear

My stomach bounced with each note!

Record yourself singing staccato. Have your buddy listen, too

FLEXIBILITY IN SONGS

When you feel like these exercises are easy, begin with riffs or coloratura in songs. You may need some time with the exercises—a few days or a few weeks—or you may feel good in ten or fifteen minutes. Just remember this isn't a race. This is a journey.

RIFFS

Practicing riffs has three challenges. First, you've got to be able to hear the notes and intervals. The best way to learn to do this quickly and efficiently is to listen to *small* sections. That's why you learned the previous scales, so you could train your voice to move while keeping your larynx and the surrounding muscles relaxed and hear all the notes. The next challenge with singing great riffs is phrasing. Phrasing means *how* you emphasize certain notes or groups of notes within a riff, either rhythmically or dynamically.

10.4 EXERCISE
How to Learn Riffs

1. Learn the notes and intervals.

Choose a riff from either "Who You Are" by Jessie J or "Lullaby of Birdland" by Ella Fitzgerald. Select something that is within your experience. It's best to begin with a riff of four to six notes. Try repeating the notes you hear. You may have to sing slowly. Keeping the recording just on that section with the riff, play it back again and check your notes. Are you able to repeat the notes? You may have to play back the recording several times to be sure. You can also use a keyboard or piano to find the notes you hear.

2. Check your technique.

Find out if you are singing the riff with a relaxed larynx, tongue, and throat. What vowel are you singing? Is it easy? Is there another vowel that would make it easier? Place your index finger under your chin, pointing up, while singing the riff. Is the area under your chin soft and still, not moving with the notes? Sing the riff on *mm* or *nn*. Can you sing all the notes clearly and easily with consistent volume? Do the notes of the riff include pitches in a difficult area of your voice? See chapter 2, pages 27–28.

3. Singing the riff with musicality.

If you've worked out the rhythm well, you should feel the direction and goal of the riff. Can you identify which notes in the riff are important to the harmony and which notes are decoration? Can you sing those notes with more rhythmic feel or more variation in the dynamics? Can you sing some of the notes in the riff as "throw away," like words in a sentence that aren't important (e.g., *a* or *the*)? Can you choose another vowel or two vowels that express the emotional idea?

COLORATURA

Singing coloratura has the same challenges as singing riffs in contemporary music but requires even greater consistency of tone. Also, the composition and the style of the song or aria will dictate some of the rhythmic and expressive choices. Sometimes a singer's musicality exceeds their vocal skill so they can get into trouble singing coloratura. I trained a young tenor who had gone through undergraduate and graduate voice programs and a few young artists programs as a bass because he was an excellent musician with a large dramatic voice. Unfortunately, years of singing only in the low range while at the same time singing musically demanding roles (he could learn an opera score in less than a week!) had taken its toll on his voice. He was completely hoarse, with a range of about five notes. He had sought out help from doctors and voice teachers but had just about given up when he came to me for a session. We were able to recover his voice and get his voice back in a tenor range, but it was very difficult for him to work slowly on his voice because of his musicianship. During one lesson, his voice was a little tired and less flexible. He told me he'd been singing coloratura arias on the weekend! Musically, he found it so easy to pick up a score and sing through long coloratura passages that he did it for fun. But unfortunately, he didn't have the stability in his voice yet, so his larynx was moving with each pitch! Although he was an excellent musician, and wise enough not to push his voice, he was singing too lightly and without even contact, so he developed tension and fatigue very quickly. It can be difficult to be patient when you are an advanced musician, but if you train your voice step by step, you will get the fastest results. Review the following songs to find out if you can sing coloratura without creating this kind of tension.

10.5 EXERCISE
How to Learn Coloratura

1. Sing Bellini's "Vaga luna."

This song doesn't really have a coloratura passage, but it is a great song to begin developing flexibility while keeping legato phrasing. Pay attention to the words that have two notes on one vowel. The first one occurs on the word *luna*. There you sing two notes on the vowel *uh*. Even though the word is written *a*, it will be easier to visualize singing *uh* to prevent the chance of singing *agh*, which would cause your larynx to rise and change the resonance.

- Can you sing the *uh* on two notes without closing your mouth when moving from one note to the next? Place your index finger on the front of your chin to find out!

- Can you sing the *uh* vowel on two notes without tightening your tongue? Place your index finger under your chin pointing up to find out!

- Find the other words in the text that have two notes on one vowel. Practice singing those words without closing your mouth on the second note or tightening your tongue.

2. Sing Handel's "Bel piacere"

This song requires more flexibility. Can you sing the words that have several notes on one vowel with the same technique you used in "Vaga luna"?

- In this song, you can also practice managing dynamics on each phrase, which will improve flexibility and prepare you for longer coloratura passages. Can you sing the repeated phrases at different volumes?

Singing riffs and coloratura are skills every singer can learn. When you have the freedom to move your voice without sacrificing your tone or comfort level, you have considerably more choices for expressing emotion in song. Great composers and great artists know how to use moving notes to add emotional emphasis to the message of the music and lyrics. Although there is always an element of showmanship when singing a great riff, jazz improv, or Mozart coloratura passage, it is important to remember the raison d'être! What is the emotional message?

A flute, piano, guitar, or violin can move through a wide range of notes quickly and impressively. A skilled singer can be just as impressive, but there is a difference: the humanity and message of the lyrics. Singers should not be trying to imitate a piano or violin just to sing a lot of notes! There would be no need for a human voice if that were the primary focus. Instead of thinking about singing notes, focus on what you want to say. What's the message? Great singers choose to add ornaments, riffs, improvisation, or even just a few notes on special words based on the attitude or emotional idea they want to express. Nat King Cole, Adam Lambert, Diana Krall, and Kelly Clarkson are examples of singers who do this very effectively. When you tactilize, audicize, and visualize the message, the notes will take care of themselves.

LESSON ROUTINE B

I used to work in the cotton fields. There were a lot of African Americans . . . a lot of Mexicans—the blacks, whites, Mexicans, all out there singing, and it was like an opera in the cotton fields . . . I can still hear it in the music I write today.

—Willie Nelson

You've reached the final lesson routine. Even though this routine is more advanced, you have all the tools, concepts, and strategies you need to successfully develop and maintain your singing. Depending on your previous experience and the condition of your voice, you may not be ready to forge ahead with this routine. You may want to use the previous routine a bit longer, or you may want to mix and match. This is your journey, so you should follow your own pace. And since conditions for your voice change, you may be recovering from a cold, a big performance, or a break from singing, so you may want to return to the first exercises. You should continue to do different exercises according to what you need at any particular time. And, don't forget, have fun!

VOICE TRAINING

Remember to TAV. Use your experience to help you choose the best scales for you. If you don't feel comfortable with any scale, refer to other scales in the book that you enjoy.

- 4.1 Octave-and-a-half arpeggio on lip rolls
- 3.3 Descending five tone
- 3.1 Triad with repeating octave
- 3.4 Triad without consonants
- 6.2 Octave-and-a-half arpeggio on *mum*
- 7.1a Triad with octave repeat on *ney*
- 7.1b Octave-and-a-half arpeggio on *ney*
- 10.1 Broken Octave on lip rolls and *oo*
- 7.3 Octave-and-a-half arpeggio on *oo*

LISTENING TRAINING

Listening to great singers provides you with a model for a voice that can move easily from low to high, with clear vowels and consistent contact, no matter what style of music you sing.

1. Pick a song from the recommended list below and listen to the whole song.

2. Print the lyrics, text, or score.

3. Write on the printout where you notice dynamics, vowels, tone.

4. Go back and listen to the "money" notes, large intervals, or the chorus of each song.

5. Write on the print what vowels and dynamics you hear in those sections.

Female Contemporary and Musical Theater

Beyoncé, "Love on Top"
Kelly Clarkson, "Low"
Jessie J, "Who You Are"
Kelli O'Hara, from *The King and I*, "Hello Young Lovers"
Sutton Foster from *Little Women*, "Astonishing"

Male Contemporary and Musical Theater

The Beatles, "Yesterday"
"Empty Chairs at Empty Tables" from *Les Misérables*
Adam Lambert, any songs from the concert tour of Queen
Michael Bublé, "Home"

Female Classical

Montserrat Caballé, "O mio babbino caro" from *Gianni Schicchi*
Eleanor Steber, "Porgi amor" from *Le nozze di Figaro*
Marilyn Horne, "Una voce poco fa" from *The Barber of Seville*
Grace Bumbry, "Sequidille" from *Carmen*

Male Classical

Bryn Terfel, "Se vuol ballare" from *Le nozze di Figaro*
Luciano Pavarotti, "Una furtiva lagrima"

SONGS FOR YOU TO SING

Practice the skills you've learned in a new situation. Choose a song from the preceeding list. You can even choose one from a genre you don't typically sing. Follow the steps here one at a time. You may need two or three days on each step. Can you apply the training to music?

1. Print the lyrics/text to the song.

2. Read the words out loud. Find the meaning of each word.

3. Circle the words that are the most meaningful to you.

4. Circle the words that convey the main message of the song.

5. Reread the example from chapter 9 and apply it to your song.

6. Write the vowel sounds you hear on the important words.

7. Learn the song by singing the melody on lip rolls instead of words.

8. What are the most difficult sections? Where are the difficult intervals? When do you have to go up and then back down in pitch range? Remember *tactilize*, *audicize*, *visualize*.

9. When you know the melody, sing it on text/lyrics. Manage dynamics and the vowel shape.

10. Reassess. If you're having difficulties, practice the difficult sections using *goo* or *ney* or your favorite sound.

Chart Your Experience

Answer yes, no, or don't know.

_____   The song felt easy to sing

_____   Inhale was calm without any gasping

_____   Sounds consistent throughout the range

_____   Felt uncomfortable on the higher notes

_____   Sound of my voice changed at the higher notes

_____   Quiet on the lower notes

_____   Consonants feel easy and sound clear

_____   Dynamics are easy to manage

Record your song on video. Watch the video, and if you have a trusted buddy, friend, or family member, ask them to watch with you. Answer the questions again.

REFLECTIONS

- How did you physically feel singing the song?
- Which skills worked for you? Even volume? Consistent tone?
- Which skills didn't work for you?
- What would you like to change about the way you sing the song?
- Which exercises would help you make the change?

AFTERWORD

When I began writing this book in the winter of 2018, I envisioned a solid training manual with practical, real-world tools and strategies designed to reach singers who want to solve challenges. If you've been reading the stories and interviews, working on the scales and charts, and really thinking about the questions, you've reached a point where your sensory awareness is far greater than you ever imagined it could be. You've opened a whole new world you may have not accessed in the past, or at least not to the degree that you can now. Your toolbox is full, and you know how to use it. When you're in a coaching session, rehearsing, performing, or recording, you have choices: audicize tone and tuning using vowels and lip shapes, increase intensity by tactilizing the "funny" or pharyngeal sounds, inflect the lyric or phrasing to communicate more emotion, accept that anxiety is part of your instincts, but have courage to trust your own experience.

Now, I have a new vision. I see this book as just the first step toward a more powerful approach to living your life. You see, developing sensory awareness empowers you to make better choices about singing so you can respond to vocal demands easily and authentically. But it doesn't stop there. When you're living in your own experience, you grow more confident, the effects of past traumas are weakened, making decisions is easier, celebrating is more fun, and you have a strong defense against critics because your own experience is your truth. You're not bound by "rules," you're not trapped by unconscious habits, and you're not shackled by insecurity. You can respond authentically to your environment and the events around you.

You can see how this works in nature by watching animals. While scuba diving, I see many wild marine animals and watch their behavior more closely than possible on land. (Marine animals either ignore you or play with you.) Each species has their own personality, strengths, and weakness, and they respond naturally to their environment. Striped bass are the "boss" of the New England shore—they are quite confident and quickly show up on the scene whenever they think food might be easily available. They circle around scuba divers for a long time, chasing skates and flounder when they can see them under the sand. Giant turtles seem to be aware of their size, and they're quite content to float along slowly, ignoring everyone else, as if they own the entire ocean and every other living thing is totally insignificant. Seals are freewheeling partiers—they just want to play and have a good time as long as they're in shallow water, staying together in packs like dogs, and hoping you'll give them a belly rub. Sharks are special. They are quite serious. They seem to know their size and they move through the water like a torpedo on a mission. They know where they're going and no one is going to get in their way. But there's something they all have in common: each animal is responding to their sense of their environment. Quite naturally, they live according to their sensory awareness, using their own tools and strategies to make choices effortlessly. Humans can live their lives the same way, and great artists have mastered this way of life. Whatever your personal style, whether you're a seal or a shark, you can reach your goals and visions for your life and singing when you are aware of your environment and have the courage to respond.

This even affects your music career. Whether or not you can make a living or a good income as a singer depends on many factors, a great deal of which are beyond your control. But when you're audicizing, tactilizing, and visualizing the world around you, you're able to recognize opportunities and make good decisions. Remember the birds who master their skills because the survival of their species depends on it? This is your mission, too. Persistently focus on mastering your craft, no matter how formidable the obstacles may seem, as if the survival of your species depends on it. This is how you'll find yourself and your voice, so you can share your message with the world for the rest of your life.

NOTES

INTRODUCTION

1 Seth Riggs, ed. John Dominick Carratello, *Singing for the Stars, a Complete Program for Training Your Voice*, rev. ed. (Van Nuys, CA: Alfred, 1998).

CHAPTER 1: MOBILIZE YOUR VOICE, MIND, AND BODY

1 Birgit Nilsson, *My Memoirs in Pictures* (New York: Da Capo, 1981).

2 Nilsson.

3 See Richard A. Schmidt and Timothy D. Lee, *Motor Learning and Performance: From Principles to Application*, 5th ed. (Champaign, IL: Human Kinetics, 2014).

4 Carolina Labbe and Didier Grandjean, "Musical Emotions Predicted by Feelings of Entrainment," *Music Perception: An Interdisciplinary Journal* 32, no. 2 (2014), 170–185.

5 Joseph LeDoux, *Anxious: Using the Brain to Understand and Treat Fear and Anxiety* (New York: Penguin, 2016), 216.

6 Marilee J. Bresciani Ludvik, ed., *The Neuroscience of Learning and Development* (Sterling, VA: Stylus, 2016), 48.

CHAPTER 2: DISCOVER *WHAT* NEEDS TRAINING

1 Jaime Kautsky, "Begin with the End in Mind: Tips, Tools to Evaluate Diamond Rough," Gemological Institute of America, January 14, 2016, https://www.gia.edu/gia-news-research/begin-end-mind-tips-tools-evaluate-diamond-rough.

2 Kautsky.

3 The International Phonetic Alphabet (IPA) is a standard spelling of language sounds created in the late nineteenth century. IPA is used by speakers and singers to correct

speech problems, learn foreign languages, and improve diction. Classical singers learn IPA so they can easily learn to sing in many languages. See https://en.wikipedia.org/wiki/International_Phonetic_Alphabet.

4   James A. Stark. *Bel Canto: A History of Vocal Pedagogy*,(Toronto, CA: University of Toronto Press, 2018), 86.

5   Stark, *Bel Canto*, 122–127.

6   Ingo R. Titze, "The Science Behind Semi-occluded Vocal Tract Exercises" (presentation, International Voice Teachers of Mix, Salt Lake City, UT, 2016).

7   Ingo R. Titze and Katherine Verdolini Abbott. *Vocology: The Science and Practice of Voice Habilitation* (Salt Lake City, UT: National Center for Voice and Speech, 2012), 198.

8   Stephen Daw, "Idina Menzel, Kristin Chenoweth & the Cast of *A Very Wicked Halloween* Look Back on 15 Years of *Wicked*," *Billboard*, October 24, 2018, www.billboard.com/articles/news/broadway/8481510/idina-menzel-kristin-chenoweth-wicked-interview.

9   "Wade in the Water" is an example of a song written to communicate with people along the Underground Railway to guide them along the route, https://en.wikipedia.org/wiki/Wade_in_the_Water.

CHAPTER 3: CONNECT THE LOWER AND UPPER RANGES

1   Elias Leight, "Quincy Jones Looks Back on the Making of Michael Jackson's 'Bad,'" *Rolling Stone*, August 30, 2017, www.rollingstone.com/music/music-features/quincy-jones-looks-back-on-the-making-of-michael-jacksons-bad-117216.

2   Lars Riecke, Mieke Vanbussel, Lars Hausfeld, Deniz Başkent, Elia Formisano, and Fabrizio Esposito, "Hearing an Illusory Vowel in Noise: Suppression of Auditory Cortical Activity," *Journal of Neuroscience* 32, no. 23 (2012): 8024–8034.

CHAPTER 4: EXTEND THE CONNECTION

1   Ludvik, *Neuroscience of Learning and Development*.

2   Jennifer Ackerman, *The Genius of Birds* (New York: Penguin Books, 2016), 157–158.

3   Ackerman, 171–185.

4   Denise C. Park, Jennifer Lodi-Smith, Linda Drew, Sara Haber, Andrew Hebrank, Gérard N. Bischof, and Whitley Aamodt, "The Impact of Sustained Engagement on Cognitive Function in Older Adults: The Synapse Project," *Association for Psycological Science* 25, no. 1 (2013): 103–112.

5 Titze and Abbott, *Vocology*, 10.

6 Steven Brown, Elton Ngan, and Mario Liotti, "A Larynx Area in the Human Motor Cortex," *Cerebral Cortex* 18, no. 4 (2008): 837–845.

CHAPTER 5: WHAT ABOUT BREATHING?

1 André Gide, *The Counterfeiters* (Nouvelle Revue Francais, 1925).

2 Mary Helen Immordino-Yang, *Emotions, Learning, and the Brain: Exploring the Educational Implications of Affective Neuroscience* (New York: W.W. Norton, 2016), 103–104.

3 Johns Hopkins School of Medicine, Interactive Respiratory Physiology (encyclopedia), accessed January 2018, http://oac.med.jhmi.edu/res_phys/Encyclopedia/Menu .HTML.

4 Mary Massery, "Musculoskeletal and Neuromuscular Interventions: A Physical Approach to Cystic Fibrosis," *Journal of Royal Society of Medicine* 98, no. S45 (2005): 55–66.

5 Joseph Jordania, *Why Do People Sing? Music in Human Evolution* (Tbilisi, Georgia: Logos, 2011).

6 Jason Beaubien, "Why Elephants Pose a Threat to Rohingya Refugees," WBUR News, April 17, 2019, https://www.wbur.org/npr/712415430/why-elephants-pose-a-threat -to-rohingya-refugees.

7 LeDoux, *Anxious*, 53–58.

8 Jaak Panksepp and Guenther Bernatzky, "Emotional Sounds and the Brain: The Neuro-affective Foundations for Music Appreciation," *Behaviourial Processes* 60, no. 2 (2002): 133–155.

CHAPTER 6: REFINE RESONANCE

1 Joseph C. Stemple, *Voice Therapy: Clinical Case Studies,* 2nd ed. (San Diego: Singular, 2000) 428–429.

2 Gabriele Wulf, "Attentional Focus and Motor Learning: A Review of 10 years of Research," *Bewegung und Training* 1 (2007): 22.

3 Matthew Beard, "Jagger Takes Up Singing Lessons to Preserve Voice," *Independent*, August 10, 2006, https://www.independent.co.uk/arts-entertainment/music/news /jagger-takes-up-singing-lessons-to-preserve-voice-411249.html

CHAPTER 7: WHAT ABOUT POWER?

1   Edgar F. Herbert-Caesari, *The Voice of the Mind* (London: Alma Caesari-Gramatke and Rolf Gramatke; Robert Hale, 1978), 333–354.

2   James A. Stark, *Bel Canto: A History of Vocal Pedagogy* (Toronto: University of Toronto Press, 2008) 322–333.

3   Ingo R. Titze, "What Makes a Voice Acoustically Strong?," *Journal of Singing* 61, no. 1 (2004): 63–64.

4   Kristina Simonyan, "The Laryngeal Motor Cortex: Its Organization and Connectivity," *Current Opinion in Neurobiology* 28 (October 2014): 15–21.

CHAPTER 8: BROADEN PERSPECTIVE

1   Lady Gaga, live television appearance, *One American Appeal,* October 21, 2017.

CHAPTER 9: EXPRESSION AND INTERPRETATION

1   "The Contentious History of the Happy Birthday Song," *All That's Interesting*, June 27, 2016.

BIBLIOGRAPHY

Bigelow, Robin T., and Yuri Agrawal. "Vestibular Involvement in Cognition: Visuospatial Ability, Attention, Executive Function, and Memory." *Journal of Vestibular Research* 25, no. 2 (2015): 73–89. doi: 10.3233/VES-150544.

Brown, Steven, Elton Ngan, and Mario Liotti. "A Larynx Area in the Human Motor Cortex." *Cerebral Cortex* 18, no. 4 (2008): 837–845. doi:10.1093/cercor/bhm131.

Fitch, W. Tecumseh. "The Biology and Evolution of Music: A Comparative Perspective." *Cognition* 100, no. 1 (May 2006): 173–215. https://doi.org/10.1016/j.cognition.2005.11.009.

Habibi, Assal, and Antonio Damasio. "Music, Feelings, and the Human Brain." *Psychomusicology: Music, Mind, and the Brain* 24, no. 1 (2014): 92–102.

Henderson, W. J. *Early History of Singing.* New York: Longman, Green, 1921.

Herbert-Caesari, E. *The Voice of the Mind.* London: Alma Caesari-Gramatke, 2002, First ed, Robert Hale, 1951.

Hoch, Matthew, and Mary J. Sandage. "Exercise Science Principles and the Vocal Warmup: Implications for Singing Voice Pedagogy." *Journal of Voice* 32, no. 1 (2018): 79–84.

Juslin, Patrik. "From Everyday Emotions to Aesthetic Emotions: Towards a Unified Theory of Musical Emotions." *Physics of Life Review* 10, no. 3(2013): 235–266.

Kleber, Boris A. and Jean Mary Zarate. "The Neuroscience of Singing." *The Oxford Handbook of Singing.* Edited by Graham Welch, David Howard, and John Nix. Oxford: Oxford University Press, 2014. https://dx.doi.org/10.1093/oxfordhb/9780199660773.013.015.

Kreutz, Gunter. "Does Singing Facilitate Social Bonding?" *Music and Medicine* 6, no. 2 (2014): 51–60.

Panksepp, Jaak, and Guenther Bernatzky. "Emotional Sounds and the Brain: The Neuro-affective Foundations of Musical Appreciation." *Behavioural Processes* 60, no. 2 (2002): 133–155.

Riecke, Lars, Mieke Vanbussel, Lars Hausfeld, Deniz Başkent, Elia Formisano, and Fabrizio Esposito. "Hearing an Illusory Vowel in Noise: Suppression of Auditory Cortical Activity." *The Journal of Neuroscience* 32, no. 23 (2012): 8024–8034.

Stanislavski, Constantin. *An Actor Prepares.* New York: Theater Arts, 1936.

Stark, James A. *Bel Canto: A History of Vocal Pedagogy.* Toronto: University of Toronto Press, 1999.

Titze, Ingo R. "What Makes a Voice Acoustically Strong?" *Journal of Singing* 61, no. 1 (2004): 63–64.

Tokuhama-Espinosa, Tracey. *Mind, Brain, and Education Science.* New York: W.W. Norton, 2011.

INDEX